ESSENCE
OF THE
TAROT

Modern Reflections *on* Ancient Wisdom

MEGAN SKINNER

New Page Books
A division of The Career Press, Inc.
Franklin Lakes, NJ

ESSENCE OF THE TAROT
EDITED BY NICOLE DEFELICE
TYPESET BY EILEEN DOW MUNSON
Cover design by Lu Rossman/Digi Dog Design
Printed in the U.S.A. by Book-mart Press

To order this title, please call toll-free 1-800-CAREER-1 (NJ and Canada: 201-848-0310) to order using VISA or MasterCard, or for further information on books from Career Press.

The Career Press, Inc., 3 Tice Road, PO Box 687,
Franklin Lakes, NJ 07417
www.careerpress.com
www.newpagebooks.com

Library of Congress Cataloging-in-Publication Data

Skinner, Megan, 1958-
   Essence of the tarot : modern reflections on ancient wisdom / by Megan Skinner.
      p. cm.
   Includes bibliographical references and index.
   ISBN 1-56414-748-7
   1. Tarot. I. Title.

BF1879.T2S59 2004
133.3'2424--dc22

                                                                                2004040876

This book is dedicated to all Seekers of Truth.

Acknowledgments

Many heartfelt thanks to family, friends, clients, and associates who, each in their own way, made significant contributions to this book.

Special thanks to:

Andrea Hurst, Brigitte Labouvie and Angie Kitchin, whose wisdom and loving support made this book possible.

TABLE OF CONTENTS

INTRODUCTION

T o the uninitiated or skeptical, the Tarot may seem to be nothing more than a deck of simple picture cards with no apparent purpose or meaning. But to those willing to open their minds and imaginations, these cards become much more. The Tarot represents a journey into an ancient world of spiritual knowledge. Although created in antiquity, its wisdom is timeless, and now possibly more relevant than ever before. In today's changing world, the Tarot can be an integral guide and a useful tool in gaining insight into one's own life choices incorporating a bigger, spiritual perspective.

The cards are the way we access the knowledge of the Tarot. Each image represents a specific life experience, both universal and deeply personal. Ultimately, a deck of Tarot cards is an invitation to one's own self-discovery.

> So don't be timid.
> Load the ship and set out.
> No one knows for certain
> whether the vessel will sink
> or reach the harbor.
> Just don't be one of those merchants
> who won't risk the ocean!

—From *Work in the Invisible* (Rumi)

Using cards comprised of images and symbols, the Tarot makes an invisible world visible. These eternal archetypes have a life of their own and stimulate recognition deep within our subconscious. Like a book of historical photographs, the Tarot presents characters and stories that may seem foreign, but somehow familiar at the same time, pictures that stir memories and compel us to dig deeper into our psyche for meaning and answers. We consult the cards when seeking answers—and this is appropriate, for the Tarot is a wise oracle. The images of the Tarot form a mysterious pictorial language. They are keys into a state of awareness and insight that cannot be described by the limitations of mere words.

The Tarot is a visual medium that stimulates the imagination. Oswald Wirth, in *The Tarot of the Magicians,* describes the Tarot as "a true alphabet of the imagination," saying further that "to divine is to imagine rightly." It is unfortunate that in modern times the word "divination" carries so much negative baggage, such as fortune telling, prophecy, even sorcery, when divination is an act of intentionally connecting to the Divine. All the knowledge in the world is of little matter if we cannot apply it in our everyday lives, to the present and possible future. It is through the art of divination that we learn about the cards, and it is as much an art as storytelling or painting.

Although there are many theories and legends, no one knows the true origins of the Tarot. Perhaps the most compelling explanation is that the cards originated in ancient Egypt and were designed as a series of lessons for those being initiated into the Egyptian Mysteries. To enter into the Mysteries was to enter a select and sacred world. Some believe that the images of the Tarot, specifically what are now known as the 22 cards of the Major Arcana, were presented as doorways that an initiate passed through—a process in which the seeker actually experienced the essence of each card or lesson. When each doorway was passed through, the initiate was said to hold an understanding of the very mystery of life. Whether this is truth or simply legend, the thought is hopeful, that in aligning oneself with the image of a Tarot card there is the possibility of enlightenment.

The question then becomes, how does one now make these pictures speak? This is the initiation. Understanding the cards requires a certain amount of technical and historical knowledge. Some mystics have dedicated their lives to an academic exploration of the Tarot. A foundation of knowledge is important, for it is from this foundation that we master the complexity of the cards. Yet there comes a moment where their complexity becomes simplicity, when learning becomes experience: a sudden eureka, an epiphany and awakening. This is the moment we strive for.

Though this technical understanding is important, those who are most schooled in the Tarot know that interpreting the cards is more art than science. It comes from a combination of the rational (or intellectual) mind and the creative (or intuitive) mind. Once we put into place a structure of technical knowledge, the creative mind is given free rein to explore. Ultimately, a true discovery of the Tarot requires a willingness to surrender oneself to the power of one's intuition.

Intuition is the ability to sense that of the non-physical realm: thoughts, feelings, and impressions. By nature, we humans are intuitive creatures. We all have a psychic or intuitive muscle, often called the third, visual, or mind's eye. Like any muscle, the more you exercise it, the stronger it will become. Imagination is the capacity to visualize the non-physical. In discovering and mastering the Tarot, imagination and intuition go hand in hand.

Chapters 1–4 of this book examine the background and history of the Tarot, its relevance in your life, and different ways to use the cards. Chapters 5 and 6 present two different views of the cards themselves. Chapter 5 explores the ancient yet timeless symbolism of the 22 images of the Tarot's Major Arcana. It contains references to early systems of knowledge applied to the Tarot, including astrology, mythology, the Kabbalah, and mysticism. It focuses on the more spiritual and meditative aspects of each card and includes a traditional divination for each as well.

Chapter 6 is like a diary that draws on my personal experiences with the cards and on insights gained while working with clients. It includes references to literature, film, and daily life in the 21st century.

These stories help to make the cards real and alive, taking them out of the realm of metaphysics and into everyday reality. It encourages you, the reader, to develop your understanding of the cards by applying them to modern life and your own personal experiences.

My relationship with the cards has been a continual process of discovery, both technically and personally. I received my first deck of Tarot cards when I was 14 years old, and as I have evolved in my own life, so have my perceptions of the cards. I think you will find that the Tarot grows with you. The cards are not stagnant images, but illustrated mirrors that can reflect your own journey of discovery and self-exploration. That it is an open book, open to one's own unique perspective and interpretation, is the beauty and magic of the Tarot.

1

Welcome to the Tarot

Mysterious Beginnings:
A Brief History of the Cards

The Tarot deck we see today includes 78 picture cards divided into two sections: the Major Arcana and the Minor Arcana. This book focuses on the 22 cards of Major Arcana, or the Trump cards as they are sometimes called. Both Arcanas have significance but, as will be revealed, each is quite different with its own particular and distinct purpose.

The word Arcana comes from the Latin "arcane" meaning secret or mystery. ("Arcana" refers to the Major and Minor card groups. "Arcanum" is used to apply to the individual card.) The origins of the Tarot are appropriately shrouded in mystery. Different versions of the cards show up throughout time and history in places as diverse as Persia, Asia, Greece, Egypt, and Western Europe. Many Tarot scholars have debated their beginnings, each with their own theories and agendas. In actuality, there is no tangible proof of their origins. As the cards themselves can be, their beginnings are elusive.

Most agree, however, that the Tarot was created in an ancient era, a time that pre-dates the birth of Christ. In this ancient world there was an underground religious movement called "the Mysteries," a mystical religion that originated in Egypt. Initiation into the Mysteries was a process of personal enlightenment that was said to profoundly transform one's state of consciousness. Some of our most esteemed philosophers, mystics, and great thinkers including Socrates, Plato, and Pythagoras were initiates into this ancient spiritual sect.

The Mysteries were closely associated with the Gnostics. Gnosticism is an esoteric religion that was as much a part of the popular culture as Christianity, Judaism, and Buddhism are today. Both the Mysteries and Gnosticism were based on pagan beliefs, spiritual folklore, the movement of the planets, goddess and deity worship, and were in opposition with the growing power of the state-run church. Gnostic means "knowing," as in the pursuit of coming into a direct knowledge of God. The Gnostics, like the initiates of the Mysteries, were dedicated to a deeper understanding and exploration of the meaning of human existence.

There were two levels of participation in the Egyptian Mysteries: the Inner Mysteries and the Outer Mysteries. The Outer Mysteries were accessible to everyone. They were based on ancient myths passed on from generation to generation and expressed through storytelling, ritual, and simple magic. On the other hand, initiation into the Inner Mysteries was more select. We must remember that, in olden times, to go outside of traditional church doctrine could result in dire consequences—persecution and, in some cases, even death. Thus the teachers of the Mysteries used symbols and imagery as an encoded secret language for their mystical teachings.

To engage with the Inner Mysteries was to consciously choose to enter a secret and sacred process where the initiate strove to become at one with the myth presented. The ritualistic use of symbols and pictures was an essential part of this process. Initiation involved deep introspection and meditation during which the seeker symbolically and psychically entered into, and interacted with, the mystery or lesson presented. Simply put, the metaphor, parable, or allegory was transformed into an actual experience of knowing.

In my experience, the Major Arcana represents the purpose of the Inner Mysteries. These cards are possible doorways into a higher state of consciousness. Within their rich imagery lie timeless tools for self-discovery, both in perceiving inner truths and in the realization of our connection to a higher cosmic order. The cards of the Minor Arcana are more aligned with the purpose of the Outer Mysteries. They serve as a form of storytelling. Whereas the Major Arcana focuses on spiritual truths, the Minor Arcana are more contemporary by design and relate more to outside circumstances of day-to-day life.

A hypothesis, one that comes from both study and personal intuition, is that the two Arcanas of the Tarot originated separately. I have come to believe that the images of the Tarot, specifically those that have become the 22 cards of the Major Arcana, were fundamental teaching tools for those being initiated into the Mysteries. They are the spiritual foundation on which the Tarot is based. Like many, I adhere to the notion that the Tarot was born in Egypt, the home of the Mystery schools, most probably in Alexandria. One can only wonder what profound knowledge was taken from us in the burning of the great library that once stood there. The Tarot has survived and prospered through many incarnations, evolving into the deck of 78 cards in use today.

Certain legends say that the Gypsies brought the Tarot to the European continent as they migrated west from Egypt. The Minor Arcana, the remaining 56 cards of the deck, were first documented in 14th century Europe. At this time, Tarot cards came into vogue in the courts and aristocratic circles as a fortune telling game. It is perhaps this fortune-telling aspect of the cards that has led to so much superstition regarding the Tarot's purpose. Divining the future can be one expression of the cards, yet I do not believe that this was the original creator's intent.

Some postulate that the cards of the Minor Arcana were the precursor to our modern day playing cards. Both have four suits: cups (hearts), wands (clubs), swords (spades), and pentacles or coins (diamonds). Both card sets also contain aces, kings, queens, and knights (jacks), although there are no pages in playing cards.

The Tarot of modern day is essentially two separate decks, each Arcana having value for different reasons. In the Tarot's evolution, some of the images have changed according to the times and the different interpretations of the authors. For example, The Hierophant sometimes becomes The Pope, The High Priestess turns into The Popess, The Magician originally (to some) was The Juggler, and The World is now often called The Universe.

Systems of Knowledge:
Numerology, Astrology, and the Kabbalah

Just as there are many opinions about the Tarot's origins, there are as many theories on how the cards apply to different systems of spiritual knowledge, most notably astrology and the Kabbalah. The Tarot is an entity within itself. It is not *based* on either system, yet there are shared common themes.

As the Tarot cards are comprised of pictures and images, their meanings can prove elusive, and there is often a need to explain by association. Correlating them with sympathetic systems of spiritual knowledge assists us in defining the cards in a fashion that is helpful in interpretation. The integration of mystical sciences, as well as academics, is an important aspect of not only the Tarot's evolution, but of all sciences. Each contains ancient fundamental truths and by marrying their different elements, we gain a depth of perspective that has been lost through time.

Numerology: Numbers are some of the most ancient symbols known to humankind. They are the basis of all esoteric teachings. Each card of the deck is numbered and carries the vibration and meaning of its assigned number.

Astrology: From early time, the ancients used the practice of associating the signs of the Zodiac and their corresponding planets with the Tarot. Now astrology is the most familiar system used. It receives emphasis here because, in my practice, I have found astrology to be particularly useful in understanding the cards. For specifics see the *Astrological Table and Paths* section of this book.

The Kabbalah
(Qabalah, Cabala):

The Kabbalah is a traditional form of Jewish mysticism. The Kabbalists make a compelling argument for linking the Tarot with the pathways, or sephiroth, of their Tree of Life. One aspect of their argument is that the Hebrew alphabet has 22 letters and aligns in a synchronistic manner with the 22 cards of the Major Arcana. The Hermetic Order of the Golden Dawn (of the late 19th century) in particular put much emphasis on this association, which originated with the work of mystic Antoine Court de Gebelin. Golden Dawn leader MacGregor Mathers and later (and more controversial) member Aleister Crowley took this tradition to new heights. Their work has greatly influenced how we see and interpret the cards today.

Modern psychology is the latest development in applying new and different sciences to the cards. The introduction of Jungian psychology in particular has given us a new avenue through which to explore the cards and apply their meanings to modern life. Another important voice on this journey has been Joseph Campbell. His thoughtful interpretations involving the integration of different facets of mythology, psychology, spiritualism, anthropology, and storytelling have been instrumental in weaving together a tapestry of elements that is timeless. Campbell, a gifted storyteller, has carried on the ancient tradition, bringing the past into the future in a way that is nothing short of enthralling.

These mystical systems and their modern psychological counterparts are helpful tools in exploring the Tarot, especially as starting points and spring boards to understanding and interpreting the cards. The ancient symbolism of the Tarot is universal and is reflected in elements of life all around us. It can be seen in different aspects of nature, the arts, and literature. Your personal experience with the cards can become its own system of knowledge. Being open to discovery and using intuition as your guide will reveal the Tarot's wisdom in many amazing and different ways.

2

HOW THE CARDS WORK

The Tarot and its sister oracles, the I Ching of Asia and the Runes of Scandinavia and the British Isles, are all methods of connecting to ancient knowledge. Each is tailored to the cultural beliefs of the regions they sprang from, and all share a foundation of symbols and numbers, which are the basis of all esoteric teachings. Where the Tarot defines itself and is unique is that it reveals its wisdom through the timeless language of imagery.

Robert Wang says in *The Qabalistic Tarot*, "The cards are Astral images, illustrating the world of matter below, and symbolically reflecting the worlds of mind and spirit above." Pictures and images, or archetypes, as Carl Jung describes them, carry the vibration, the actual energy or essence, of the image presented. Just as some primitive tribes believe that photographs capture the soul, the pictures and images of the Tarot can be like imprints or mirrors of the soul's journey through life.

There is an ancient Celtic term called *scrying*. Scrying comes from the word "descry," which has several meanings: to catch sight of something difficult to discern, to know through divine inspiration or, most simply, to reveal. Mystics have used the technique of scrying for centuries in understanding symbols and discerning their meanings. It can be a useful tool in gaining a deeper understanding of the cards of the Tarot. Scrying is a method of projecting an inner vision of self. This process is accomplished through meditative exercises that engage the imagination and one's intuition in a state of becoming one with an image of focus. This is a psychic process where one's sense of divine knowing interacts with the image. Ultimately, there is an inner experience and comprehension. For example, as I wrote about each card, I experienced an uncanny synchronicity with them in my life, and truths about each were revealed to me in many ways. Writing this book was another step in my own journey of initiation into the mystical and mysterious ways of the Tarot.

Mysticism is based on the presence of unseen and impenetrable truths outside of ourselves. To truly engage with and understand the Tarot, one must become a spiritual detective willing to explore the very mysteries of life, to become a mystic in a sense. Symbols are timeless guides to understanding deeper truths—both universal and personal in nature. They spark recognition deep within our psyche and unconscious mind in a way that cannot be explained in words. The symbols of the Tarot are based on ancient spiritual truths, giving us a way to connect with the bigger picture and a deeper understanding of our lives.

Each card of the Tarot represents a specific life experience and spiritual lesson. There are two ways to work with the cards. The first method requires meditation on the card you wish to explore. I have found this to be the most profound method in gaining insight into the cards. This is an intuitive process that engages one's sense of inner knowing and wisdom. Because the symbols of the Tarot are timeless, within us all there is an unconscious understanding of each card. By quieting the mind and focusing on the image, insights will come to you. This may happen in the moment or may come later as you go about the activities in your life. The intuitive process cannot be rushed, as patience is a part of the journey toward understanding and wisdom. It is helpful to keep a journal to record your insights and perceptions.

The second way to understand the cards is through the practice of divination. Divination is a way of applying the meanings of the cards to a specific question or aspect of life you wish to explore. It can be done by asking a question and choosing a card to give you the answer or by doing a reading using a card spread. The divination process can give you a lot of information about a specific element of your life. In the process, you will also gain a deeper understanding of the cards. To do your own readings, consult Chapter 4 of this book. Both the meditative and divination methods are appropriate and useful in gaining understanding about the cards and your life, so choose the method that most resonates with your situation.

Choosing Your Deck

There are hundreds of Tarot card decks on the market today to choose from, some traditional and others less so. The cards come in a wide variety, from decks based on ancient themes such as the Renaissance and Medieval times, to decks with more modern caricatures. Each deck carries the imprint of the author's and designer's perceptions. They are artistic interpretations of the symbolism of the Tarot. Like a painting in a museum or art show, some decks will reflect more of your personal taste than others. A deck of cards will call to you just like a painting you love and admire. Ultimately, the right deck will mirror something deep inside of you.

Perhaps you have heard that one should never buy their own deck of cards, instead they must be given to you as gift. This belief comes from the olden times when magic was seen as a gift to be honored and is a part of the tradition of sharing and passing on knowledge. But as this practice is somewhat impractical today, it is best to take the bull by the horns, so to speak, and buy your own deck.

This book uses the Universal Tarot. This deck is traditional in appearance, but has a modern feel. I believe it expresses the timelessness of the cards well. The Universal deck is extremely popular today because it is both beautiful to look at and clear and easy to understand. You can, however, apply the interpretations and definitions presented here to any deck and gain similar results.

Trust your intuition to guide you in this process of choosing the deck that is right for you. With time and practice, you will develop a relationship with your deck, leading you to an understanding of the imagery that will be unique to you and the deck you are using. And remember, your deck is meant to be used, not stuffed away in a drawer or old box somewhere. As in any relationship, the more you engage with it, the more you will come to know it.

3

Astrological Table and Paths

The 22 Cards of the Major Arcana

raditionally, each card of the Major Arcana is assigned a corresponding astrological ruler. The ruler defines the celestial quality of each card. Rulers are signs of the Zodiac, planets, or elements.

In the cases of The Fool, The Hanged Man, and Judgment, there is both a planet and an element. This is because these cards are associated with the outer planets—Uranus, Neptune and Pluto—which were discovered in the late 18th and early 19th centuries. Before this time, the ancients had only an element—Air, Water, or Fire—to apply to each card. Now it is commonplace to use both the element and planet to define these cards.

The Path is a key word that describes the essence of each card. It is the singular focus and experience of each Arcanum. The ruler is the planet associated with each card. The chart on page 26 illustrates both the ruler and path for each Arcanum.

	Card	Ruler	Path
0	The Fool	Air/Uranus	Liberation
I	The Magician	Mercury	Discipline
II	The High Priestess	Moon	Contemplation
III	The Empress	Venus	Love
IV	The Emperor	Aries	Authority
V	The Hierophant	Taurus	Divinity
VI	The Lovers	Gemini	Discernment
VII	The Chariot	Cancer	Achievement
VIII	Strength	Leo	Heart
IX	The Hermit	Virgo	Wisdom
X	Wheel of Fortune	Jupiter	Opportunity
XI	The Hanged Man	Water/Neptune	Surrender
XII	Justice	Libra	Balance
XIII	Death	Scorpio	Endings
XIV	Temperance	Sagittarius	Alchemy
XV	The Devil	Capricorn	Fear
XVI	The Tower	Mars	Destruction
XVII	Star*	Aquarius	Inspiration
XVIII	Moon*	Pisces	Darkness
XIX	Sun*	Sun	Joy
XX	Judgment	Fire/Pluto	Reckoning
XXI	The World	Saturn	Wholeness

* Paths 17, 18, and 19 are the Luminaries of the Tarot deck: The Star, Moon, and Sun. By definition, a Luminary is both a source of light and one who illustrates any subject or instructs humankind. The Star is Creative Light, The Moon is Reflected Light, and The Sun is Revealed Light. Just as in numerological practice there are the master numbers 11, 22, and 33, the Luminaries are somewhat separate domains from the other cards. They are significant because they represent the most challenging and the best of what can be achieved in an individual life. They could be described as Master Paths. The Luminaries represents those who are teachers and instructors. They are motivated by a desire to make significant change not only in their own lives, but in the lives of others.

4

Divination:
Readings and Card Spreads

Divination is the process of divining, or foretelling a probable future. It is a process of discovery through perception and insight. Most simply, it is asking a question and seeking an answer. A card layout or spread can give you a more comprehensive understanding of a situation or aspect of your life than just one card. A spread is like a story unfolding. The cards interact with each other to give you a fresh perspective on your situation, a view that incorporates different elements, giving you a more complete picture than you may not have been aware of previously. Included here are some different spreads. You can also make up your own layout depending on the situation you wish to explore.

Although it has become a popular practice to read an image that is right side up as having a positive meaning and an upside down (or reserved) card as negative, this is not necessarily the case and can be confusing to the reader, especially in regards to the larger context of the reading. Each card carries both the positive and negative elements of each Tarot archetype. It is up to you to discern or divine what this will mean. Doing a reading is largely an intuitive process, using your imagination to perceive and weave together different possibilities or scenarios.

What I have found is that when a card appears right side up in a reading, it represents the truest and strongest expression of the image. These cards tend to be more forceful in their expression. Cards that are reversed or upside down can reflect the more introverted or subtle essence of the image. They can be more tentative in their expression. But again, it is up to you to decide what works for you. Remember, your decision about the process will set up the interpretation.

Before doing a reading, it is important to set the intent. This means taking a moment to become clear and centered, focusing on the matter you wish to be clarified and the spread that you are using. Taking a deep breath or two will help. Shuffle or mix up the cards. Then either spread the cards out and intuitively pick the number of cards indicated, or cut the cards into three piles, pick a pile, and choose the appropriate number of cards from the top.

The Destiny Spread

The Destiny Spread can be used to explore your destiny (or path), representing your Divine course or purpose in life.

1. Soul (Past). This card represents the inherent gifts that you were born with. It is your deepest self, incorporating your memories, secret dreams, and the inner workings of self that make up your personal nature. It may also represent the area where you get blocked or stuck in the comfort of the past—relying on the old.

2. Spirit (Present). This card represents your vital essence, the qualities of self that are in a state of evolution and development as your life unfolds. It is the expression of the self in the here and now. It represents new or unrealized talents or abilities that have yet to be fulfilled—what needs to be activated.

3. Destiny (Future). This card is a combination of the Soul and Spirit, representing your path or Divine purpose. It is your big picture: the infinite possibilities of self that are activated by inspiration—your wishes and dreams for the future. A good way to look at this placement is as a goal that you are working towards achieving—what needs to be embraced.

The Lovers Spread

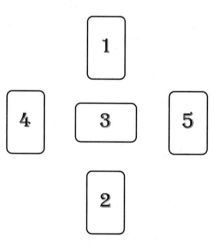

This spread explores your relationship with another. It can be helpful in understanding the nuances, problems, and possibilities of a relationship in your life.

1. You in regards to the relationship. This card represents your expectations, your hopes and desires for the relationship.

2. The subject of your inquiry. This card is how the person of your inquiry perceives you, what you represent to them.

3. How you engage with one another. This card can be interpretated in two ways, either that which blocks or hinders the relationship, or what helps to move the relationship forward.

4. The foundation. This card represents your past together, the foundation for the relationship.

5. Probable outcome. This card represents your possible future together.

The Moon Spread

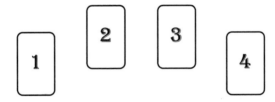

This spread is based on the different phases of the moon. A lunar cycle represents a beginning, middle, and end for a specific period of time. The Moon Spread can be used to reflect a process of development of an idea or situation in your life.

1. The New Moon: the beginning of a new cycle. This card represents a time to plant the seeds of new dreams—your intent.

2. The Crescent or First Quarter Moon: a time for clarification. This card represents a need to decide what works and what doesn't. Focus on nurturing and development.

3. The Full Moon: The situation reaches its apex or full development. This card represents what you need to let go of—a time to be at peace.

4. The Waning or 4th Quarter Moon: Darkness before rebirth. This card represents what to expect next—the process of preparing for the new cycle.

The Astrology Wheel Spread

The Astrology Wheel Spread is based on your natal birth chart. The natal horoscope is your nativity, representing your life story. It is a road map to the infinite self. Obtaining your birth chart is easy; there are a number of online sites where it can be purchased or your local astrology or metaphysical bookstore may offer the service of running charts.

This spread uses all 22 cards of the Major Arcana and intertwines them with your natal chart. It can help you understand your horoscope and how the cards work in your life story. Each card of the Major Arcana is ruled by either a sign of the Zodiac or a planet. Here we apply them to their specific placement within your birth chart. The 12 cards ruled by signs of the Zodiac would be applied to the house ruled by the sign. For example, The Emperor is ruled by Aries so you would place this card in the house that Aries rules in your chart. The other 10 cards of the Major Arcana are represented by planets. As an example, The Magician is ruled by Mercury and would be applied to the placement of Mercury in your chart.

An example of the Astrology Wheel Spread using John Lennon's natal chart is shown on page 34.

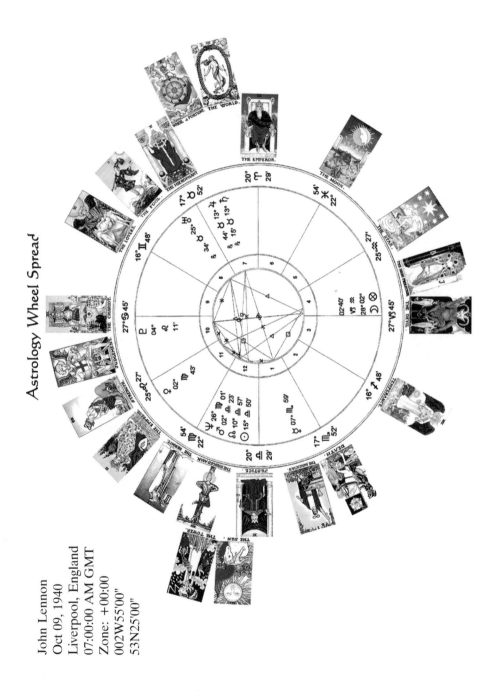

Astrology Wheel Spread

John Lennon
Oct 09, 1940
Liverpool, England
07:00:00 AM GMT
Zone: +00:00
002W55'00"
53N25'00"

Houses

1st: Self, outer persona.

2nd: Money, possessions, self worth.

3rd: Siblings, communication, early education.

4th: Home, family, roots.

5th: Creativity, children, self-expression.

6th: Health, work and service.

7th: Relationships: significant other, partnerships.

8th: Transformation, sex, shared resources.

9th: Philosophy, religion, higher education, travel.

10th: Career, reputation, reputation.

11th: Friends and associations, future visions.

12th: Spirituality, unconscious, collective.

5

ANCIENT WISDOM

o—The Fool

Path of: Liberation
Ruler: Uranus
Element: Air

Salvation, whatever salvation may mean, is not to be obtained on any reasonable terms. Reason is an impasse, reason is damnation; only madness, divine madness, offers an issue.

—Aleister Crowley

he Fool wears many faces and may appear to us through a variety of different guises. This is because The Fool is a trickster and a shape-shifter. He is savior, criminal, jester, madman, holy man, and divine child. The Fool exists today in modern playing cards as "The Joker"—the wild card. The Joker can upset a king, trump an ace, and generally cause havoc wherever he appears. The Fool's motto is: expect the unexpected. It would seem only fitting that there is some controversy surrounding The Fool's placement in the Tarot deck. The Fool's number is "0." So does he belong at the beginning, at the end or, as some would profess, between the 20th and 21st Arcanum, between Judgment and The World?

This is an academic argument for which The Fool, in essence, has little inclination. The Fool has no home. He is a nomad, a wandering vagabond, free to travel into our lives when and where we have the need to be liberated from old ways of thinking and being.

Uranus rules The Fool. The connection between the two becomes apparent starting with Uranus' eccentric orbit: revolving around the sun on its side. Uranus represents originality, invention, and independence. This planet serves to awaken us to our creative uniqueness. Uranus is often called "the earthquake planet," and for good reason, as it loves to shake things up and disrupt the status quo. Uranus functions through rebellion. The Fool rebels against all established authority. He obeys a higher order—absolute inspiration—the space where miracles are just waiting to happen.

Before Uranus was discovered (in the late 18th century) the element of Air was attributed to The Fool. The Fool symbolizes pure Air: the realm of ideas and inspiration before they are grounded in time and space. In the realm of Air, all things are possible, and ideas can flourish before they are limited by form. The Fool defies all limitations; he is formless and ever changing. He represents that sublime and blissful state where we are foolish enough to believe in all possibilities.

The Fool's number "0" symbolizes the great void, the cosmic abyss. In this abyss lies all creativity not yet born. To enter this realm and explore its unlimited treasures, The Fool takes on the persona of eternal child. The child is innocent, blissfully unaware of any consequences to his actions or of the future. The Fool appeals to the child within us as all. He represents the folly associated with youth and of the eternal spring. In springtime, we feel free—whether stimulated by nature, or the sheer joy and wonder of discovering the unknown—to act on our most primitive urges. The Fool encourages us to fling ourselves with total and reckless abandon into whatever inspires us in the moment.

A simple definition of this card is *action beyond all reason.* This card can be interpreted in two ways: as a model and as a warning. On one hand, The Fool represents the transcendence of intellect in the name of spirituality or inspiration. Through his ignorance, The Fool becomes divine because in his folly he dares to go where even angels fear to tread. Yet on a practical level, his irresponsible ways make him somewhat of a criminal; his actions are outside of the laws and bounds of normalcy. The Fool walks the fine line between inspiration and insanity. Is he holy man or madman? It is up to you to decide. Crowley says of The Fool: "This queer stranger? Let us entreat him kindly. It may be that we entertain an angel unawares."

Ultimately, The Fool's journey symbolizes the initiate's journey into the Tarot. In a sense, as The Fool travels through the deck, so do you. Those who choose to enter its mysteries are required to be fools, to let go of any and all pretense of reason, to be totally open and fearless to what you may find.

Divination

Look out! If The Fool has appeared to you, be ready to experience profound change. This card represents a quantum leap forward in your life and the beginning of a whole new way of thinking and being. This is a time to be open and spontaneous, to take a vacation from doubt and worry, to play the fool and allow yourself to be and do whatever inspires you in the moment—and damn the consequences! The Fool offers no guarantees, especially in regards to outcomes. Yet, if you dare to embark on his path, to risk his folly, he offers transformation in the sense that you will never be the same again. Have faith. When in doubt or feeling fearful repeat this mantra: "The Fool jumps off the cliff because he knows the angels will catch him. I am The Fool. The Fool jumps off the cliff...."

1—The Magician

Path of: Discipline
Ruler: Mercury

When every cell of your body is so present that it feels
vibrant with life, and when you can feel that life every
moment as the joy of Being, then it can be said that
you are free of time.

—Eckhart Tolle

The Magician is the first card of the deck, and perhaps the most significant, for he holds the key to all of the Tarot's mysteries. Just as the ancient mathematicians (some would call them our first magicians) believed that numbers were sacred and contained the secrets of being, The Magician possesses the formula to the very essence of creation. On a symbolic level, he is the creator; his number is one, representing creative power and the beginning of all manifestation.

Manifestation is a process of sustained effort or energy; it is the will directed towards an intended outcome. For some of us, manifestation does not always come easily, but what The Magician tells us is that it can be learned. Manifestation first requires courage, then effort, concentration, and, a key element to this card, *discipline*. The Magician is part scientist, part mystic, and part artisan. He takes the potential of The Fool and crafts it diligently and thoughtfully— much as one would solve a math equation, or strive to understand a Buddhist koan (or riddle), or sculpt a piece of clay—into an actual means of expression.

The Magician has been called "Le Bateleur," The Juggler, for he is learning the art of balancing different abilities or tools. The Magician's tools, his instruments of magic, lie on the table before him: a wand, a sword, a cup, and a pentacle. The wand represents desire; the sword, intelligence; the cup, imagination; the pentacle, the physical body, the vessel for manifestation. The tools can be interpreted as different talents or capacities that are in a state of development. We do not see The Magician in the act of juggling for at this moment it is happening solely in his mind. The mind is his learning ground. Because he is able to think it, ultimately, it becomes real.

The Magician's ruler is Mercury, an Air planet symbolizing the mind. In mythology, Mercury is often characterized as a deity with winged feet, here manifested in the lightness of The Magician's being and process. His genius lies in his dexterity. With the concentration of a practiced juggler, The Magician is able to control all the elements and keep them in the air like a juggler's balls, seamlessly, as if there is no beginning and no end. The Magician is joyously at one with his process and, for a moment, he makes us believe that it is easy.

Magicians are masters of illusion. Magic is tricking the mind into a suspension of belief in the properties of time and space. Simply, magic is mind over matter. Some philosophers would tell us that life is an illusion. An ancient Chinese parable beautifully illustrates this concept: "Am I a man dreaming of being a butterfly, or butterfly dreaming of being a man?" It comes down to a matter of perspective. On the Magician's path, we realize the illusion and begin to make it our own.

Astrologically, Mercury rules all forms of communication. The phrase, "in the beginning was the word," is often associated with The Magician, symbolizing the first act of creation. To evoke words, spoken or written, is to transmit energy or ideas into actual form. Mercury is known as the Messenger of the Gods representing the God-given ability within us all to create our lives. Thoughts have power and words are spoken thought. The Magician reminds us that they will greatly shape the reality we experience.

The Buddhist masters speak of Zen as a state of consciousness where one is said to become aware of the infinite possibilities of being, a state that is only achieved by quieting the mind. Consciousness is in the present moment. Thus said, The Magician can be calculating in his process, which should be used in serving the greater good. All else is deception and manipulation.

A simple definition of this card is *as above, so below*. When we become at one with the eternal flow, we reach a state of conscious fluidity.

Divination

Imagine that there is no past and no future, only now, the present. The ability to fully embody the present moment is the power of The Magician. It is in present time that all true creation begins. This card represents a time of new beginnings, the start of a creative process, or of a new endeavor in your life. You have the tools and may now feel inspired to develop and learn how to use them in a whole new way. This will require letting go of all distractions and focusing on the tasks at hand. Be specific about what you want to create, as your intent is the foundation for all that will become. You're learning as you go, so find joy in the process. Life is your initiation; see through the illusion and recognize your creative power.

43

II—The High Priestess

Path of: Contemplation
Ruler: The Moon

I early arrived at the insight that when no answer comes from within to the problems and complexities of life, they ultimately mean very little. Outward circumstances are no substitute for inner experience.

—Carl Jung

Whereas The Magician represented the first step in the act of creation—"I *think* therefore I am," The High Priestess is the second step, the *knowing* of the act. What is the difference between thinking and knowing? It is the difference between light and shadow, reason and faith, words and images; it is the difference between the sun and the moon. The High Priestess is ruled by the Moon. She wears a lunar crown and knows it is in the mystery of the night that her power lies.

The High Priestess is seated and holds an open book upon her lap. Compare her position to that of The Magician, who is pictured standing and looks to be in the middle of a performance. The High Priestess sits passively telling us that, unlike The Magician, there is no action required on her path. If she were to have a task it would be to receive. Perhaps the most difficult of actions is in conscious non-action, in the willingness to sit quietly and to listen. The High Priestess waits in silent expectation to receive her answers as they are revealed from within. She represents the sacred axiom: "Ask and ye shall receive." She has mastered the art of all great mystics, the art of *contemplation*.

The book that has so captured our High Priestess's attention that she seems to be in a state of suspended rapture is the Book of Knowledge (or Secrets). She is the guardian of this sacred book. There are many books of knowledge: the Bible, the Torah, the Koran, the Book of Runes, and the I Ching. The Tarot, with all of its secret teachings and rich imagery, is like a great picture book of knowledge. Pictures and images, unencumbered by the limitations of words, are our purest connection to profound knowledge.

Myrna Lofthus, in her book *A Spiritual Approach to Astrology*, describes the moon as a symbol for "the sum total of all the personalities one has been from previous incarnations." These previous personalities and lives combine in this path to increase our awareness, becoming a multifaceted knowledge. Maybe you have had the sensation of remembering something from another time and place that existed before you were born, or have looked into the eyes of a perfect stranger and felt the eerie chill of recognition, or have had a premonition of something that will happen. Then you have traveled within the timeless domain of The High Priestess. She possesses eternal knowledge: the memory of all things past, present, and future.

The Akashic Records is a theosophical term used to explain this phenomenon. The Akashic Records refers to a universal filing system that is said to record one's every thought, word, and action. These records are impressed on a subtle substance called Akasha, meaning all-pervasive space. Much like cosmic fingerprints or DNA, these records represent the imprint of one's very soul. A simple definition of this card is *intuitive knowing*. Within each of us is knowledge of the potential of all things.

The moon reflects the light of the sun. It represents the earth's soul. When the waters of the moon are stilled, they provide a perfect mirror to reflect our deepest selves, our soul. In traditional astrology, the moon is a symbol for mother. In ancient times, The High Priestess was worshipped as spiritual mother. To the ancient Egyptians, she was Isis, the goddess from whom all Becoming arose. She was the mother of God, the creator of the Divine, and it was through her knowledge that God learned the mysteries of the stars. Yet because of her knowledge and her ability to give life (her feminine power), The High Priestess was seen as threatening to the hierarchy of the male-based church. Often she was labeled crazy, insane, even persecuted as a heretic or witch. Today, The High Priestess, present within all of us, is here to help right the imbalance of male and female in spirituality and religion—to bring the eternal into the present.

In Kabalistic teachings, The High Priestess is represented by the letter Gimel, meaning "camel." This amazing beast has the ability to travel great distances while holding gallons of water in its stomach. There is a tale told about an ancient group of travelers lost in the desert. Desperate and near madness from thirst, they killed their camel and drank the water from its stomach. Are we all not thirsty for water as we journey through this sometimes desert wasteland of life? The High Priestess represents a well for us to drink from, that of the great eternal ocean known as the soul.

Divination

This is a time to go within and nurture your soul through meditation and deep contemplation. You may find yourself experiencing a heightened state of awareness, in touch with a consciousness that is an extension of your present reality. Remember, the intuitive realm does not always line up in a linear manner; it is an extra fold of perception. Trust your senses, your feelings, and your intuitions, whatever comes to you in the moment. Let them reveal to you what you need to know. Breathe through each moment with its gift of reflection. You are in a process of "deep remembering." If your sense of memory brings you sadness, it may be that you are experiencing an "eternal sadness." Blessed are those with the gift to cry. Cry the tears of the moon.

III—The Empress

Path of: Love
Ruler: Venus

True love is nothing but a certain urge striving to fly up to the divine beauty.

—Marsilio Ficino

The Empress is one of the most popular cards of the Tarot deck. Like her ruler Venus—a planet so brilliant that it is often called a star—The Empress radiates a luminous intelligence, and we cannot help but be dazzled by her light. The Empress wears not so much a crown as a tiara of jewels or stars representing the 12 stars of creation or the 12 signs of the Zodiac.

Venus is the planet that inspired the childhood rhyme: "Star light, star bright, first star I see tonight. I wish I may, I wish I might, get the wish I wish tonight." The Empress inspires our wishes, our desires, and the promise of all creativity.

In astrology, Venus rules two signs: Libra and Taurus. Libra represents the *airy* qualities of this planet, our ideals of beauty and love. Taurus, the *earthy* aspect of Venus, epitomizes the sensual and tactile. Libra appreciates beauty intellectually, like a connoisseur discussing fine art. Taurus is more Bacchus-like: a fabulous dinner party with good food, good friends, and lots of wine. The Empress incorporates the Venusian qualities of both signs—the rational and the passionate; it is the principle of pleasure in all its forms.

In Greek mythology, Venus is known as Aphrodite, the Goddess of Love and Beauty, who enticed both men and gods alike. Venus and The Empress relate to the archetype of Eve in the Garden of Eden. Eve was sublimely naughty. She conversed with the Serpent, ate the "forbidden fruit," and tempted Adam. The Empress is confident in her sensuality, her ability to give life. She is open and welcoming and feels no need to protect herself.

The Empress also represents mother, or motherhood, a creative process in itself. The Empress is the earth mother, as compared with The High Priestess, the spiritual mother of the Tarot. Both cards represent the feminine, but each is different in its expression. The High Priestess fits the image of the Madonna: virginal and enigmatic. The High Priestess looks rather austere, even intimidating, her consciousness pristine and, in a sense, untouched. She has chosen the Veil of Isis, a cloak of mystery to protect herself.

The Empress card as a symbol of motherhood may translate to relationships with our own mothers. This relationship is our first experience of the feminine. In a psychological sense, the mother relationship is the most primal and complex of all. It affects the quality of all our future relationships, greatly shaping our ability to love both others and ourselves.

Traditionally, the mother is the nurturer, the giver of comfort, love, and support. In the purest sense, The Empress represents *unconditional love*, the highest of all love, given without expectations. When out of balance, The Empress can be an over-protective and possessive mother, an over-giver. For some, The Empress may represent our mothers' unfulfilled desires.

A simple definition of this card is *the wisdom of love.* Through this path, we explore our capacity to give and receive love. This process involves learning a balance between heart and mind, a balance of self and other. Ultimately, The Empress represents the capacity to nurture and support us in equal proportion to the ability to nurture and support others.

The Empress could be described in terms fitting the quality of a Renaissance painting. The Renaissance was a time when astrology and the arts flourished, where artists and philosophers looked to the heavens and the celestial bodies for insights into the human condition. The artist Sandro Botticelli was an individual inspired by the spirit of Venus. Indeed, the Goddess of Love became his muse. Botticelli's paintings show voluptuous women, often naked, frolicking in nature and the elements. The Empress is a sensual celebration of nature and of life. She is comfortable in her body, for it is in her body that she experiences love's many pleasures.

The Empress then is love, in regard to both its celestial and terrestrial aspects. Her number is three, representing body, mind, and spirit. Here, the path to the Divine is through the gift of the body: Where love and desire become art itself.

Divination

The light of love shines brightly within you. As you become more comfortable with yourself and your life, your confidence will attract others to you. You deserve love but you must decide what quality of love you wish to receive. Enlightenment comes from a feminine wisdom, the ability to make wise choices. This is a time to take a step back from the "busy-ness" of life: Stop and smell the roses and experience all that you have created. Be proud of your creations, no matter how big or small. They are like flowers in a garden and, with love, they will blossom and grow. Nurture yourself, your body, and your senses. For now, pleasure is not a luxury, it is a necessity. Love is all around you, so partake generously, and then abundance in all its many forms will surely follow.

IV—The Emperor

Path of: Authority
Ruler: Aries

We should conduct our lives as though we were kings
and queens with all eternity before us.

—Eliphas Levi

T he Emperor's path is a majestic one, as well it should be, for here we become symbolic kings, the masters of our domain. Yet it is not always easy to be king. The Emperor wears a heavy crown, representing *authority,* and with it, the burden of responsibility. Authority is a divine right; how we choose to deal with it is another matter. At his best, The Emperor is a powerful ruler, a leader who acts with the greater good of the kingdom in mind. When out of balance, he becomes domineering, controlling, and authoritarian—a tyrant.

Aries, a Fire sign and the first sign of the Zodiac, rules The Emperor card. Aries implies *beginnings*, symbolizing the assertion of the individual ego (fire) as it strives to separate from source. Mars, the mythological "God of War," in turn rules Aries, here fighting against the collective pull of the past and helping us to individuate. The Emperor is the archetype of warrior. He is the original warrior engaged in the ultimate battle—the battle to be.

In astrology, Mars is the masculine principal, male energy, representing the urge for action, the desire to create self. The Emperor, potent and all-powerful, is pure male energy. We all have a male and female side, not necessarily in a sexual sense, but in regards to our larger psyche. The Emperor card symbolizes the way in which we express our male energy.

Robert Wang defers to the wisdom of the *Golden Dawn* text in his description of The Emperor as "the general, the conqueror, hot, passionate, impetuous." In history, we have many examples of the warrior/emperor's dark side, namely of his abuse of power and his aggression. The Roman Empire was built (and destroyed) during the astrological period of Aries. The Emperor Napoleon is a classic example of warrior-energy run amuck. His was a case of conquering for the sake of conquering, where the need for ego gratification overtook wisdom and reason. This is a tradition that unfortunately continues in the world today.

Yet the emperor we see here holds no weapon. He is not going into battle. This emperor is seated on a stately throne of granite or stone, on solid ground. He does not rule by the sword, but by his scepter—a crucial distinction. His scepter, like his crown, represents authority. The Emperor is an imposing figure: regal, powerful, and dynamic. He has earned his power and, most importantly, he has owned the responsibility of it. It is through this ownership that others naturally respect and respond to him. He rules, not through force, but by the sheer nature of his presence. Here we learn the fine art of governing and keeping the peace, of how to lay down the law and set clear boundaries, even if becoming a leader means that you will displease some.

The Emperor is also a symbol of our paternal role model. In a psychological sense, "father" represents how we make our way in the external world, the world of form. The Emperor represents the ancient rite of passage from father to son (or daughter) where we become responsible for not only our lives, but the lives of others as well. A simple definition of this card is *personal sovereignty*. In dignifying self, you give dignity to others. Authority requires discipline, assertiveness, patience, and teamwork. By adhering to these qualities, you become worthy of wearing The Emperor's crown.

The Emperor's number (four) represents *foundations*. On this path, we create the foundations for our "kingdoms," our business empires, which we will build into careers. This is an excellent time for conquering new business enterprises. In these endeavors, The Emperor is energetic and forceful while at the same time providing a stabilizing influence. This requires an instinct for knowing when to act and when not to act—the mark of true leadership.

Divination

You have reached an auspicious moment in your life. This is the time where you take to your throne of personal empowerment. How you conduct yourself now is of great importance; others are looking to you for leadership. Act with integrity toward yourself and others. Issues may now arise with males in your life, specifically authority figures: your father, mentor, partner, or boss. This is a circumstance where you may feel someone is trying to dominate you, or you have to defend your turf. However, this is not a time for battle. Do not act impetuously. Take a step back, center yourself, and remember that if you are truly powerful, no one can take it away from you. New enterprises in business thrive, as you are full of energy to create your kingdom. You are laying important foundations for the future. Pay careful attention to follow-through.

54

V—The Hierophant

Path of: Divinity
Ruler: Taurus

*When leading, be generous with the community,
honorable in action, sincere in your words. As for the
rest, do not be concerned.*

—The Buddha

The Tarot has survived many incarnations and variations, according to the current historical and political climates. In olden times, often the only way to pursue one's mystical nature was through the sanctuary of church. Hence, many of our greatest esoterics and mystics were Catholic priests. In fact, in some decks The Hierophant is known as "The Pope." Before the rise of Christianity, "Hierophant" (Reveler of Sacred Things), was the distinction given to the High Priest of the Eleusian Mysteries. Whatever his title, the figure portrayed in this card represents a seemingly infallible presence. He is a leader and a shepherd of Divine law.

The Hierophant is shown in the act of benediction: the giving of divine blessings. He represents our earthly connection to higher spheres, to heaven and God itself. The Hierophant is a conduit, the intermediary between the human and the Divine. He is the embodiment of spiritual father, the person or authority whom we trust with spiritual matters and the keeping and well-being of our soul.

"Father, pray for me." To minister to the soul of another is both an awesome and daunting responsibility. The previous card, The Emperor, also represents father. Through the emperor/father, we mastered authority and its natural expression of leadership. In The Hierophant, we take leadership to the next level—the ability to influence and advise others on their spiritual journey. The Hierophant could be summarized in this way: the recognition of one's worldly spiritual power and the desire to express it externally.

A simple definition of this card is: *Spiritual Teacher*. Throughout the ages, there has been a tendency to put our spiritual leaders on a pedestal. This is to assume that they are somehow above us. This practice has nothing to do with spiritual empowerment. Instead, it becomes a turning over of one's own individual power in a misguided attempt to connect with the Divine. Any spiritual authority, no matter how elevated, is by the very nature of his (or her) incarnation still human and still fallible.

This path challenges our beliefs and ideals about those we trust and look to for spiritual guidance. It warns us to watch for false prophets and teachers and reminds us not to surrender our individual power. As Liz Simpson states in *The Book of Chakra Healing*, "a spiritual teacher is not a human being trying to be spiritual, but a spiritual being learning vital emotional lessons by wearing the cloak of humanity." A spiritual teacher is learning the lessons of divinity though the conscious experience of finding the sacred in everyday life and in everyone.

The Hierophant is a communion between the individual and the Divine; it is the relinquishing of individual will to Divine will. Divine will is a detachment from outcomes, the willingness to surrender a situation or problem to a higher power. Here we sacrifice ego to become an empty vessel pure of agendas and expectations. As we let go of material concerns and become empty and open, we are in a position to receive spiritual abundance. The gifts of spirit are rich and plentiful. Here we learn the true meaning of value, the sense of security that comes from an active communion with spirit.

Taurus, an Earth sign, rules The Hierophant card. The element of Earth represents the physical-material plane, specifically the body. The Hierophant signifies the point where spirit becomes flesh: the unification of body, mind, and spirit. This is a union in search of a beloved and a fitting prelude to the next Arcanum, The Lovers. On a mundane level, this card can translate to the union with another and may present itself when one is contemplating sacred vows and contracts, such as marriage.

Taurus is a fixed sign: conservative, traditional, and above all else, stable. Here, it translates to an enduring and rock-solid spiritual foundation we can count on. It is our church, fulfilling our need to belong and ground with others in the pursuit and exploration of a connection to the Divine.

Divination

We all have the potential to be spiritual teachers, and this path may take many different forms. Sometimes being a spiritual teacher simply involves having an open heart and an open mind, and the willingness to acknowledge someone else's journey without judgment. You should strive to make even the most trivial encounter a positive learning experience. In the process, you will find that you receive as much as you give. This is spiritual abundance. Now is a time where you are seeking a connection with your spiritual community, an extended spiritual family where you can share ideas and celebrate the gifts of spirit. Know that your good intentions for others are greatly appreciated and engage the spirit in a way that is prosperous for all.

VI—The Lovers

Path of: Discernment
Ruler: Gemini

In this house of mud and water, my heart has fallen into ruins. Enter this house, my Love, or let me leave.

—Rumi

las, this is not a particularly romantic card. Such sentiments are perhaps better left to the Venus-ruled Empress, the path where love and desire meet. Gemini, an Air sign, rules The Lovers card. The element of Air can be cold, for here it represents the realm of the mind and the intellect. It is through the airy qualities of Gemini that we begin to form our ability to reason, to make distinctions and discriminate between right and wrong. Thus The Lovers represents the process of gaining discernment in your relationships.

A simple definition for The Lovers is *choice*. Typically, this card means a reality check in a relationship where a decision must be made, a choice that will greatly determine the outcome of the situation.

The story of Adam and Eve in the Garden of Eden is an obvious archetype for The Lovers. In Adam and Eve we have our first lovers and, most importantly, the first choice—paradise or sin? It is the eating of the forbidden apple, the fruit from the *Tree of Knowledge of Good and Evil* that causes the lovers to be cast out of paradise. Once they tasted the fruit, in a sense, they knew too much. It was through their awakened desire for experience that they became conscious of their nakedness, and thus their vulnerability.

We may all wish for the blissful Eden-like innocence of romantic love. Yet in romantic or idealized love there is little room for growth and learning, and The Lovers card is all about learning. This path signifies relationships, or the prospects thereof, which offer a universal, albeit sometimes painful, learning experience. In relationships, we become open and vulnerable to another—a scary proposition at times. The hook that keeps us there moment to moment, day to day, through the most difficult of lessons, is love. Without this vital, often mysterious, sometimes perplexing feeling called love, we would likely throw up our hands and abandon the whole enterprise.

What is love? Astrologer Richard Idemon describes it as "a force that brings two or more separate entities together in a way that they are totally transformed." Eros is deep and passionate love—a creative force. Through Eros we create life. And in its presence, from the heights of intimacy to the lows of longing and despair, we are transformed.

In Greek mythology, Eros is also known as Cupid, the son of Aphrodite (or Venus) who is the Goddess of Love. Cupid is a mischievous god, a trickster who shoots his arrows into the most unsuspecting of victims sending them into total disarray. Cupid may seem to strike at random, without reason, but when associated with The Lovers, we can see some purpose to his schemes. Gemini is a sign of *duality*, symbolized by the twins. Here, the rules of attraction apply. Gemini represents the exploration of self through other—the mirror of a relationship. In psychological terms this can be explained as projection, which is the projecting of one's missing self, one's unfulfilled needs and desires, onto another. Today's popular notion of finding that elusive soul mate is perhaps in reality a search for our other half, a cry for recognition, a disguised yearning for wholeness.

Commitment is not the natural forte of notoriously fickle, ever-curious Gemini. Indeed, this is often a life path issue for this sign. But a relationship, at least the deep transformative variety, requires commitment. This being a card of growth and learning, the idea of true spiritual marriage is most appropriate here. To the mystics, The Lovers card represents the alchemical marriage, a union with self that progresses into a relationship with another. Ultimately, by being complete within one's self, we are free to enter into the unknown abyss of love and be transformed in the process.

True union is a responsibility and a commitment—what happens after the honeymoon and beyond the fairy tale with all of its romantic trappings. This requires a letting go of the need for perfection or any attachment to outcome. Although challenging, this path offers the promise of great learning and the opportunity for deep personal realization. In the highest sense, the choice offered in The Lovers will bring one back to oneself. For it is rightly said that you can only love another to the degree that you love yourself.

Divination

You stand at a crossroads and a choice is before you regarding a significant relationship in your life. Think carefully. That which attracts you to another holds a magnificent reflection of your deepest desires. Do not doubt yourself. As difficult as it may be, try not to let past emotions or sentiment sway you. You must commit one way or another. Pain comes from indecisiveness. By making up your mind, you will set your heart free. Remember, there are no wrong choices, only learning experiences. Whatever your decision, know that the journey ahead will lead you to a place of greater understanding and wisdom about yourself. If you are presently unattached, you are now opening yourself up to the grand adventure of falling in love! Write down what you wish to experience with another—then let it go.

VII—The Chariot

Path of: Achievement
Ruler: Cancer

Everything in the unconscious seeks outward manifestation, and the personality too desires to evolve out of its unconscious conditions and to experience itself as whole.

—Carl Jung

ancer, a Water sign and the astrological ruler for the moon, rules The Chariot card. Moon and Water are elements associated with the unconscious. What does the unconscious have to do with the proud young hero we see pictured here, poised at the helm of his mighty chariot? A definition may be helpful. According to Webster, the unconscious is, "the part of the mind containing the psychic material of which the ego is unaware…not deliberately planned, organized or carried out." One could think about The Chariot as Cancer, the crab, emerging from the great ocean onto solid land, a process where the unconscious becomes tangible and real. This card represents your dreams becoming reality.

On a mundane level, Cancer represents home. When considered more deeply, this translates to the *home within,* the security that comes from being "at home" and comfortable with yourself. The task at hand is to take this sense of authentic self, your mobile home, into the outer world. To do this successfully, one's personal and emotional house must be in order. The crab's shell serves to protect it from outside forces and influences.

On this path, we gain a deeper sense of identity so as not to be thrown by the whims of others. Here we learn to be in charge of our journey. More than anything else, The Chariot is a test of character. Here we meet our hero, the symbolic hero that lies within us all. Joseph Campbell describes the hero's journey as a series of courageous acts, a continual process of trials and triumphs, which offer a life lived through self-discovery. The Chariot presents a challenge and an opportunity to define one's true self and character, a noble and heroic effort. The traditional meanings associated with this card, of *victory* and *success,* refer to a triumph of personal integrity in the face of unknown elements or adversity. "To thine own self be true" is a fitting motto for The Chariot.

In esoteric astrology, Cancer symbolizes the soul's point of entry into the body, the doorway into incarnation. In The Chariot is an implied birth, a new beginning, or at the very least, a turning point in one's life. This card potentiates a breakthrough of the psychic self—the inner unknown engaging with the outer world, a movement of the soul. The Chariot is the vehicle for this passage, much as the body serves as the vehicle for the expression of one's soul.

Cancer is the second cardinal sign of the Zodiac. Its cardinal qualities are personal, creative, assertive, and forward moving. The cardinal forces drive The Chariot to conquer new levels of individual achievement. We encountered the first of the cardinal signs in The Emperor (Aries), representing the path of authority. The foundation of personal authority established through The Emperor makes the journey of the Chariot possible. Without the ability to dictate one's own needs and desires, the adventure ahead would be fraught with much peril.

In closing, we end where we began, with Carl Jung. The Chariot's journey closely resembles what Jung described as the process of individuation, a process of uncovering the true self. Jung states that consciousness comes from the unconscious, and ultimately, that the whole person is a collaboration of the two. The crab is an amphibious creature; it can exist on both water and land. The wholeness of which Jung speaks is meaningful here as it symbolizes the unification of one's physical and spiritual worlds, a beginning and a completion. A simple definition of this card is *acting on intuition.*

Divination

Congratulations! Much inner-work has been done laying the foundation for a triumphant move forward. Plans previously stalled or waylaid can now be set into motion. The journey ahead will take you to many exciting new places and situations, and this in itself will challenge you. You are leaving much behind, but past experience will serve you well. You are the hero of this campaign; stand tall and do not look outside of yourself for validation or applause. If you feel the need to prove anything, then it is only to yourself. Glory comes from within. Although outcomes are not the focus here, all indications point to success in new endeavors. There is no game plan, for it would only limit you. When uncertain, take a step back and reconnect to the deep reservoir of your spirit for guidance.

VIII—Strength

Path of: The Heart
Ruler: Leo

*And there the lions ruddy eyes, Shall flow with tears
of gold: And pitying the tender cries, And walking
round the fold: Saying; wrath by his meekness
And by his health, sickness, Is driven away,
From our immortal day.*

—William Blake

ach card of the Tarot tells a story. The story of the Strength card is *The Virgin and the Lion*. There are many variations of this timeless tale, including Aesop's fable of "The Lion and the Mouse," but perhaps the most popular version of this story is "The Beauty and The Beast." A story that goes something like this...

Once upon a time, there lived a fair maiden, here called Virgo, the innocent. One day she met a ferocious beast—a lion. The maiden was both attracted to the great beast and afraid of him at the same time.

She asked herself many questions. Should she run away? Call for help to cage the beast or put him into chains? She contemplated killing the lion, but like all great stories, this is a love story, and Virgo, with her virginal gift of innocence, believed she could tame the beast and become his friend.

The Strength card is known by several names. In some decks it is called "Force," in the Crowley deck, "Lust." The lion pictured in this card is opening his mouth to the maiden Virgo. This opening, or surrender, does not happen through brute force. She is not physically capable of such an act of strength.

The heroine of our story has a compassionate heart. She is willing to believe in what others would not, namely in the lion's inherent goodness. She acts with mercy. Her patience allows her the time to know and understand the lion. Through this willingness the maiden finds herself falling in love with the fearsome creature. The result is a miracle: Virgo's love transforms the lion. Against all odds, he yields to her, without effort or struggle. This card recognizes the power of gentle strength. This is a strength that can move mountains.

The lion represents our primal animal nature. He is a symbol of passion and desire, the beast within, what we lust for. (We will meet the inner beast again in the path of "The Devil.") For many of us, lust and desire are not always comfortable feelings, often having negative associations. Yet desire is the first step in any creative process. Desire activates the vital life energy, the sacred fire, what is called the Kundalini energy or the "serpent power." This powerful force represents an initiation, unleashing our creative, psychic energy. If, like the maiden, we can learn how to cooperate with the "serpent-beast," we can reach a state of peace with ourselves,

A simple definition of this card is *kindness*. Strength comes from union, the union of mercy and desire. If you fear your passion, it will consume you much as a lion would devour a lamb. The Strength card is the path of the heart. It requires a loving act of self-acceptance. Embrace yourself, warts, fangs, claws, all of you—even the seemingly undesirable or imperfect parts.

The Strength card is ruled by Leo, the beast in our story. Leo, a Fire sign, governs the heart. The heart pumps blood, vital fluid and the energy of life, through the body. It is the source of our creative fire: what we love, our passion, what makes our heart beat fast to a timeless rhythm. Yet from an early age, many of us have been lead to believe that our desires are inappropriate or even bad. This type of conditioning takes away our creative power. The lion's fierceness comes from a wounded heart, a sense of powerlessness. This brings us to the moral of this story: Become one with your heart's desire, and like the maiden and the lion, you too will be transformed.

Divination

Have you been avoiding yourself? Perhaps you are experiencing an inner struggle, a conflict with self that makes you feel weak. The physical manifestation can be exhaustion, weariness with life. The remedy is to make peace with yourself, all of yourself. Do not force anything. Instead, be gentle and patient with yourself. Allow yourself to be vulnerable. Vulnerability is not a sign of weakness. In genuine vulnerability you will find your greatest strengths. Spend time reacquainting yourself with your passions, needs, wants, and desires. It is okay to be self-full, which is different from selfish. To facilitate your own unique process, begin to contemplate what you want in your life. This may mean lifestyle changes, as you search for a quality of life that brings you the deep satisfaction and contentment that you deserve.

IX—The Hermit

Path of: Wisdom
Ruler: Virgo

Yea, though I walk through the valley of the shadow of death, I will fear no evil; for thou art with me; thy rod and thy staff they comfort me.

—23rd Psalm of David

e begin The Hermit with a prayer, the invoking of the Psalm 23. The Hermit shown here *seems* very much alone, but remember, as you embark on this path: One never prays alone. The Hermit card presents a mysterious figure shrouded in a dark cloak. The cloak conceals The Hermit, making him somewhat invisible, and merging him with the dark night in which he travels. It is as if he is saying, "I am the night," telling us that he has not only accepted his journey, but also embraced it. He has only a single lantern to light his way in the darkness.

The symbolism here is plentiful. The cloak renders him separate and alone, in a sense, unreachable. His staff is a symbol of wisdom and intuition. Though he may not be aware, it directs The Hermit's course. The darkness represents his journey into the inner reaches of the unknown. Yet it is the lantern that is perhaps most significant to The Hermit's path. The lantern represents his faith, defined as a belief or calling to something greater than self and circumstance. Without faith, he would truly be alone. It is the light of The Hermit's lantern that both guides and comforts him on his long journey.

The astrological ruler for The Hermit is Virgo, an Earth sign. Virgo's birthday falls in the last days of summer, a time traditionally associated with the harvest, when we reap the hard labor of summer's seeds sown. The symbol for Virgo is the virgin, suggesting purity and innocence. Virgo represents the "virgin soil," the fertile ground from which wisdom is born.

The Hermit is a seeker of knowledge and wisdom. Knowledge and wisdom are two very different things. Knowledge comes from books, whereas wisdom must come from the heart. Thus the road to wisdom can be a difficult path, for true wisdom is only attained through the hard lessons and experience of time. With the virgin's purity often comes a need for perfection, hence Virgo's tendency for overanalyzing and self-criticism. But here we must rise above such tendencies to plant our seeds and trust that through patience, love, and proper nurturing, they will grow. Incidentally, these are the very lessons of the preceding "Strength" card.

This is not hope; hope is for the young and the impatient. Wisdom requires vigilance. It is a constant act of faith. The Hermit knows this, for he is wise beyond his years. He is the embodiment of an old soul.

Throughout history there have been many legends of wise souls, masters and teachers like The Hermit. One is that of the mythological wizard Merlin who guided young King Arthur to the throne of Camelot. Those familiar with the Merlin saga know him not only as a magician, but an architect, prophet, bard, and healer. Merlin followed the "old ways" of the ancient pagan or Druid sects that worshipped the Goddess and the earth. Merlin possessed many gifts, perhaps most notably his ability to connect to, and understand, the magic inherent within nature.

Both Merlin and The Hermit share a desire to serve, to help and mentor others through their own difficult processes. Hermits like Merlin work behind the scenes, sharing their knowledge, without glory, for a higher purpose, appearing to their young protégés from the shadows in times of their greatest need.

In hermetic teachings, The Hermit was one of the three Wise Men who followed the Star of David (or Bethlehem) to the manger of the Christ child. Some biblical scholars say that these wise men were actually Persian priests or magicians, likely astrologers, who divined through the placement of the stars the coming of this miraculous event. The Hermit represents the use of knowledge merged with the power of faith, a heady combination.

A simple definition of this card is *a test of faith*. Generally, this path represents a trial of one sort or another, a test of your beliefs in yourself, others, and the greater good. The Hermit's journey is a lonely one fraught with many perils, the most prevalent being isolation and despair, a feeling of being forsaken by God. True wisdom must come from within, from experience and an inner sense of knowing. By enduring the rigors of The Hermit's path, he offers the richest of rewards, the peace that comes from internal fulfillment.

Divination

If you are feeling lost or alone, do not despair. It is only by traveling into the darkness of the unknown that you will find the answers you seek. Cultivate and guard preciously your alone time. Fortify yourself with the wise counsel of those masters who have walked before you. There are teachers all around you, and guidance may come in unexpected ways—from the passage of a book, a chance meeting with a learned friend, or even in the subtle nuances of a song's refrain. You may find that you are inspired to learn and educate yourself as a way of developing your inner talents and gifts. If you have chosen this card, you have the ability to guide or serve others in some way, a worthy path. For now you don't have to share or explain your process. The Wise Man keeps his own counsel.

X—The Wheel of Fortune

Path of: Opportunity
Ruler: Jupiter

In life we cannot avoid change, we cannot avoid loss.
Freedom and happiness are found in the flexibility
and ease with which we move through change.

—The Buddha

The wheel is an ancient symbol for life itself. Each turn represents a passage of time, a new stage, and as the wheel progresses, a series of experiences unfold one after another. The Wheel of Fortune could be described as the very game of life, bringing to mind a roulette wheel and other games of chance. Here, we must be willing gamblers, ready to throw the dice or chance the wheel—to play the game or allow it to play us. The name of the game is change.

The letters TARO inscribed on the wheel may be read as ROTA, which is Latin for wheel, or TORA (Torah), signifying the Hebrew law. The Wheel of Fortune is the Wheel of Law representing the natural law of constant change. Nature is a perfect example: We experience the cycles of nature with each change of season. Each phase marks a period of time and holds a different quality of experience. On this path, we are asked to embrace the idea that change is life and life is change.

Jupiter, the biggest planet in our solar system (11 times the size of Earth), rules The Wheel. In astrology, Jupiter represents expansion and is known to be an extremely positive force. Astrologers often refer to it as the good luck planet. Jupiter functions through inspiration and its expansive energy represents a need to grow and explore new horizons. A simple definition of this card is *embracing possibility*. Opportunity is all around us, and in The Wheel of Fortune, we aspire to become brave enough to explore all of our options. Success depends upon the ability to make the most of all opportunities.

This card has been called The Wheel of Karma (or Fate), symbolizing the soul as it revolves through eternity. It turns and we are born, turns again and we die, another turn and we are born again. Karma is based on the law of cause and effect, that for every action there is a consequence. The opportunity presented in The Wheel of Fortune is the willingness to learn lessons so we save ourselves from repeating them again and again.

What makes The Wheel of Fortune spin? Duality, as the principal of polarity, of opposing yet equal forces: contraction and expansion, death and rebirth, negative and positive. This stimulation of opposites results in a counter exchange of energy, which becomes

74

perpetual motion. This can translate into both highs and lows. To calm these extremes and achieve centeredness in your life, focus on the center of the wheel. The center of the wheel is who you are now, the present you can affect. The outside of the wheel represents the unknown future with all of your fears, concerns, and stresses regarding it.

Albert Einstein once famously remarked: "God does not play dice with the universe." From a spiritual perspective, there are no accidents in life. What may seem to be luck, good or bad, could be interpreted as destiny, just as coincidence could be defined as serendipity, as the gods or a larger force at work, putting us exactly where we need to be at exactly the right moment. Even so, we are all ultimately responsible for our destinies, which are determined by the choices we make every day.

The Wheel of Fortune is represented by the number 10, symbolizing the completion of a cycle and the unfolding of a new one. In numerology, one plus zero (or 10) equals one, reminding us of The Magician (as his number is one). Both The Magician and The Wheel of Fortune are cards of manifestation, and what was begun on The Magician's path comes full circle here. Sometimes it is easier to focus on what is new, because it's exciting and different, yet it is important to finish what we started (even if it does not turn out to be everything we expected)—to harvest one's crop before new seeds are planted.

The stabilizing influence in this card is the Egyptian sphinx sitting motionless above the wheel. The Sphinx is the guardian to the gateway of the mysteries of life and death. Legend says that all who passed its threshold were required to answer a riddle or be destroyed. The riddle: "What walks on four legs in the morning, two legs at noon, and three legs in the afternoon?" The answer of course is man himself, another reminder that in the journey of life, the only constant is change.

Divination

Hang on to your hat because The Wheel of Fortune can be like a roller coaster ride. At the very least, life will not be boring. Here, flexibility is the key in all matters. You may feel like life is moving very quickly, forcing you outside of your comfort zones. This may translate to a feeling of being out of control. You cannot avoid change; instead make it work for you by focusing on the positive elements. Be grateful for all opportunities. It is up to you to make the most of them, even if it means extending yourself beyond old parameters. When overwhelmed, keep this perspective in mind: Do not to get stuck on what you cannot change. Instead, learn what you can and move on. This will free you to experience new opportunities.

XI—Justice

Path of: Balance
Ruler: Libra

It is not only the judges at tribunals who judge;
everyone judges in the degree to which he thinks. All of
us, in so far as we are thinking beings, are judges.

—Anonymous, *Meditations on the Tarot*

In the 11th Arcanum, we meet Lady Justice. Her number is significant because it represents the mid-way point in our journey through the 22 pathways of the Tarot deck. The Justice Card signals a time to evaluate our experiences thus far and reflect on the possibilities ahead. Justice wears the robes of a judge and sits in judgment of our very deeds and actions. Yet she is a fair ruler. Holding a scale, the universal symbol of law and truth, she indicates that she is honored to give a fair and balanced perspective. This card represents our inner-judge, and in the best sense, the ability to see our lives from a balanced viewpoint.

In Egyptian mythology she is Maat, the Goddess of Truth and Justice. On Judgment Day, Maat took the form of an ostrich feather in the underworld as souls passed from one incarnation into another. Upon death, one's heart is said to be placed on a scale, weighed against Maat's feather on the opposite side. Until the soul's heart becomes as light as her feather, it must repeat its earthbound journey. It is one's heart, not the mind, which is judged and determines the outcome of one's worthiness to proceed forward into the next phase of the journey.

The heart is a symbol for the center. The ancients saw it as the seat of human intelligence, calling the heart the "center of illumination." To the Egyptians, it was the indispensable center of the body in eternity. In Justice, we strive to find our center, a process involving a balance of the mind and heart. A simple definition of this card is *I think and I pray.*

Symbolizing truth, fairness, and justice, Libra, the sign of the scales, rules the Justice card. Libra is an Air sign, indicating an emphasis on the intellect; this sign loves to reason and measure, a process of weighing and balancing different sides of a situation. Justice is sometimes referred to as the great orator, debating two sides of a situation to discern the truth of the matter. Yet the desire for fairness can be a double-edged sword, as the ability to see opposite sides of a situation can sometimes lead to indecision. As we evolve through life, so will our perception of truth. Justice is shown seated between two pillars; they represent severity and mercy. She offers the grace that comes from the balance of the two. In Justice, we become supreme diplomats with the ability to embrace two different perspectives and ultimately find the middle way to peace.

In astrology, Saturn is exalted in Libra as the best expression of this sign. Saturn represents Karma and the Divine Law, reminding us of the previous Arcanum, The Wheel of Fortune. Karma is the law of cause and effect. From a spiritual perspective, it is the weighing of our actions against circumstances. In some decks, this card is called "Adjustment," representing the aspects of one's life that may need adjustment. The true state of nature is balance and individual harmony is sought one way or another, whether consciously or unconsciously. This card offers the opportunity for a midcourse correction, the ability to right our ways and past indiscretions. Thus one can regain one's center and inner-equilibrium, leading to a sense of balance.

On a mundane level, this card represents the law, which can translate to legal proceedings. This may take the form of arbitration, mediation, or the signing of contracts. In all matters, The Justice card says this is a time to be precise in your actions, to dot your "i's" and cross your "t's," to make sure your affairs are in order before proceeding onto the next experience.

Justice holds a sword—the sword of truth—reminding us of the Minor Arcana's Ace of Swords. In the Tarot, Aces represent rebirth and new beginnings, here representing a time where we may need to cut away aspects of our lives that are no longer truthful or meaningful. Although Justice encourages moderation and restraint, there are times when extreme situations require extreme measures. In this process, frankness and honest exchanges, although difficult and sometimes painful, will lead to a new sense of truth.

Divination

The Justice card represents a time to focus on the aspects of your life that are out of balance. During this time, you may have the ability to see both sides of a situation. Don't let this confuse you. This is a process of finding clarity that will help you find your sense of centeredness. Whenever possible, seek middle ground and resist going to extremes. Even if circumstances may appear to be unjust, abstain from righteous thought and action. Instead ask that divine truth be revealed to you. You can avoid major upheaval by doing this. However, if something in your life is severely out of balance, know that the natural course of events will be for the situation to right itself. The outcome will mirror the degree of imbalance. In any case, the truth at the heart of the matter will be found, and ultimately, you can expect a renewed sense of harmony in your life.

XII—The Hanged Man

Path of: Surrender
Ruler: Neptune
Element: Water

God grant me the serenity to accept the things
I cannot change, the courage to change the things
I can, and the wisdom to know the difference.

—Serenity Prayer

t first glance, The Hanged Man may seem confused, comical even, as he hangs upside down from a tree. Your instinct may be to turn him right side up and relieve his unfortunate condition. Do not be deceived. The Hanged Man is not a victim of circumstance. He has chosen this state of being. The Hanged Man shares the non-conformist nature of The Fool and presents a similar paradox: Is he completely mad or inspired by a higher calling? The Hanged Man indeed hangs from a tree, not by his neck, which would force death, but by one of his feet. In a sense, this path prepares us for the next Arcanum, Death. It is a practice run, a test, the beginning of the end to old beliefs.

The Hanged Man's heart is in the right place. He is upside down because he desires a different outlook on life. He has placed his feet in the air, the realm of spirit, because he seeks a more spiritual view: a reversal of ordinary consciousness. This card represents the need for a different attitude, a change in one's vision or perception, here representing a letting go of old material concerns and attachments. An analogy would be if you were to stand on your head and everything in your pockets (coins, etc.) would fall out. This symbolizes the release of all obstacles to achieving a higher state of awareness.

The Hanged Man looks like he is in a yoga pose, in a sense defying gravity. Yoga represents the union of spirit and self, a fitting description for this card. He is in a state of suspension, trance, or meditation. The Hanged Man is a channel (or connection) between the personality and the higher self. His is a meditation of love, a process of learning compassion for self and for others. The act of forgiveness, of letting yourself and the world off the hook, can lead to a kinder and gentler self. A simple definition of this card is to surrender without defeat. This means that you accept your innate right to feel well.

This card brings to mind the Greek myth of Sisyphus. The gods punished Sisyphus, the King of Corinth, for unintentionally betraying their secrets. Thus he was resigned to Hades and forced to roll a large stone uphill. It always rolled down again, a discouraging fate to say the least. There can be a punishing element to this card, a feeling, not always rational, of somehow having "displeased the gods," of feeling guilty without reason. This can manifest itself as a need to make things right, to gain redemption. Here one must be aware of becoming overly involved in drama, no matter how divine. The remedy is to surrender to God's will without becoming melodramatic in the process.

The planetary ruler for the Hanged Man is Neptune, in mythology, the god of the Sea. The element of Water here represents the universal ocean, the realm where all things merge or dissolve into one. In Neptune's healing waters we aspire to return to Source, the creative void from which all life emerged. Neptune's influence may result in the unconscious desire to want to return home, to the place where we are one and at peace. A dangerous effect of this need can be the inclination to check out, to not participate in life. Neptune represents the unconscious, the universal soul, and the deepest layers of the individual. It is our inner connection to spirit. In a healthy sense, it is the expression of one's spirituality in life and in our interactions with others.

This card may also bring to mind a crucifixion, images of martyrs as they sacrifice for humanity. Often historically, there has been a fine line between sacrifice and martyrdom. Originally the word sacrifice meant, "to make sacred." It was not to give up but to gain sanctuary. There are many fine lines on this path. For example, does The Hanged Man represent a sinner or a saint? He is, as we are, human, and thus embodies the qualities of both extremes. On this path, we experience the paradox of the two and ultimately the truth lies somewhere in between.

Divination

Do not beat yourself up about things that are outside of your control. Instead let go and let be. This is a time to put your trust in a higher source (or power) to resolve that which you cannot. You may experience the feeling of being completely discouraged one moment and completely inspired the next. This is the paradox of The Hanged Man. He represents the human condition, our experience as we strive to make a better life for those around us and ourselves. If your actions are based on guilt, then you may not be in alignment with your higher self. Here you do not have to make amends. However, this is not a time for complacency. Escapism, though a tempting consideration, is not your best option. When all else fails, evoke love. Leave behind mortal melodrama and find your sacred connection.

XIII—Death

Path of: Endings
Ruler: Scorpio

Why are people so afraid of death? The answer is simple. It is an unknown experience.

—James Van Praagh

Death appears here on horseback, in the guise of a dark knight. He is Cronos, Saturn, or Father Time, and he waits ready to transport us from one existence to another, an experience that could be described as the ultimate journey into the unknown. At this moment one may ask: Why me? Why now? It is important to state up front that the Death card rarely represents a physical death. Instead, this card symbolizes a death of a more subjective nature, an end to old attachments that have outlived their purpose in our lives.

This card is ruled by Scorpio, the sign of the Zodiac representing death and rebirth, and symbolizing profound transformation. Scorpio is ruled by Pluto, also known as Hades, the Lord of the Underworld. The underworld is a metaphor for the unconscious mind. Scorpio is a Water sign. In the highest sense, the element of Water represents the spirit or soul, and on a more mundane level, the emotional body.

The transformation represented in the Death card is often of an emotional or psychological nature, involving habits, compulsions, attachments, and desires that lie beneath the surface and negatively affect the quality of our day-to-day lives. The underworld is an easy place to get stuck. Yet, the scorpion has the power to transform into an eagle and fly higher than any other bird. This transformation represents the ability to experience life from a higher or more spiritual perspective.

The Winter Solstice is the symbolic death of the calendar year. With winter comes an opportunity for reflection, a time where the earth sleeps before it is reborn again in spring. Cronos (or Death) is often portrayed as a skeleton with a scythe, harvesting the old grain so it can become seed and regenerate, symbolizing the natural transition of life, here meaning a clearing away of the old to make ready for the new.

The French call sleep le petite mort, "the little death." This reminds us that we die everyday, in many different ways, and that in the span of a lifetime we experience many psychological changes. The common denominator in all things, death, birth, love, sex, or sleep, is that we are forced to relinquish control. A simple definition of this card is *letting go*. By releasing the past, you will be free to live again. Pain and suffering come from holding onto old ways of being.

The earth is the temporal plane, meaning life is temporary, a brief and fleeting moment in time. On this path, we come face to face with our mortality. Ultimately, death can give birth to a desire for a deeper meaning in life. The Death card represents a need to relinquish control, a renewed and compelling need to live more fully and value each moment.

A spiritual belief system (no matter its form) helps in navigating this path—the faith to believe that the universal plan does not give us any more than we can handle. When faced with big changes, we are forced to explore and to define our current priorities. The mystics say that within the mystery of life is an understanding of death.

Some cultures celebrate death. For example, in Latin America, the "Day of the Dead" festival acknowledges the dead and celebrates the soul's journey into another world. Theirs is a celebration of the natural cycle of life and death, a tradition that comes with dancing skeletons. The message being that by embracing death, we embrace life, and that fearing death only limits the fullest experience of life.

Dr. Elisabeth Kübler-Ross, the famous pioneer of studies on death and dying, describes the final stage of death as acceptance, that by surrendering oneself to death, there is the possibility of some peace. Ross writes, from personal experience: "The only thing that lives forever is love." Unconditional love for self transforms death into a journey of possibilities.

Divination

This is a time to breathe. Inhale and take in the new breath of life, then exhale and release the past and the old energy that has outlived its purpose. The Death card represents a time of profound change—change that will transform your life. In the process, you may experience a sense of deep loss, leaving you feeling emotionally raw and vulnerable. Grief is a natural and important part of honoring any death. To help you move on, a ritual may be in order. This could be in the form of an altar, to symbolically bring to closure what you are letting go of. Or perhaps you could try a burning ritual, where you burn old remnants of the past and release them into a greater good. Most importantly, creating time for your spiritual practice will help bring you peace. As always, time will heal all wounds. For now, mourn your endings and celebrate the new beginnings ahead.

XIV—Temperance

Ruler: Sagittarius
Path of: Alchemy

Through art *(the process of learning) the whole mass
of base metals (the mental body of ignorance) was
transmuted into pure gold (wisdom), for it was*
tinctured *with understanding.*

—Manly P. Hall

ncient alchemy was not only a science, but also a philosophy and a religion. Initiation into the *Great Work*, as alchemy was called, required direction of the mind towards an understanding of the elements of nature (human and all other) and their connection to the Divine. The participant could only understand the essence of the alchemical experiment by active participation in the process, with different levels depending on the initiate's experience. Temperance, like alchemy, represents a learning ground where you, the initiate, become a full participant in understanding the interaction of different elements in your life and how they may ultimately direct and influence its course. This is both a lofty and worthwhile endeavor, for the realization of the different ingredients in life provides the very recipe for wisdom.

The image of the Temperance card is dominated by the presence of a mighty angel. He is the Great Omnipresent Guardian Angel looking out for our best interests and protecting us on our journey through the Tarot deck. By choosing to enter into its mysteries, we are exposed to many dangers. Knowledge, whether too much or too little, can prove harmful without a foundation of earnest and beneficial intent. The guardian angel watches over us as we aspire to participate in this knowledge toward the attainment of true wisdom. His presence is an essential component of this path. Without the guiding influence of a higher order and purpose there could only be intellectual or ego gratification.

Sagittarius, the sign of the Zodiac representing higher wisdom, rules the Temperance card. Sagittarius, shooting his arrows into the sky, is the sign of the archer and the huntsman. The arrows are of directed will, representing the desire to reach into the realm of the gods in the hunt to experience the highest levels of wisdom. Sagittarius is also a centaur, the mythological creature with the lower body of horse and the upper body of a man. This sign represents the transformation of our base animal nature into the ability of the human mind to perceive and to think. Through temperance, we aspire to self-restraint. Here wisdom, the ability to synthesize experience into reason, is the great equalizer. This card translates to wisdom through experience, for without an understanding of different experiences in life we are left to the plane of simple ignorance.

The sign opposite of Sagittarius is Gemini, the ruler of The Lovers card. Temperance and The Lovers are complimentary paths because both focus on learning though experience. In The Lovers, it is Cupid that directs the course of the arrow, piercing through the lover's blissful ignorance and transforming it into practical knowledge. It was on this path that we first encountered the alchemical marriage. In The Lovers, this marriage represented the partnership with self, as well as with other, which transpired into a deeper understanding of one's true self. In Temperance, the interpretation is somewhat different. Here the alchemical marriage symbolizes the relationship between the elements of one's nature transformed into a greater understanding of the divinity within.

The Temperance card represents the combining of opposites, just as alchemy is a combination of both magic and science. The angel is seen pouring a liquid between two vessels: One is Fire (the sun) and the other is Water (the moon). In theory, these elements cannot combine, as each would extinguish the other. Here it is important to note that the alchemist's method of turning lead (or base metals) into gold was not only a material process, but also a symbolic and spiritual endeavor. In Temperance, Fire becomes Water and Water becomes Fire, combining together into a new state of being. This is a process of transmutation and synthesis. The previous Arcanum, Justice, represented the middle path of balance between two extremes; here it is the synthesis of both. A simple definition of this card is *The integration of opposites.*

The ancient alchemists used a crucible to combine their ingredients and Temperance is the crucible of transformation. This transformation comes about through not just one element, but in the combination of many. An analogy would be a conductor of an orchestra coordinating the different musicians and their instruments to create music together. One instrument would have only one sound, but together they achieve a symphony.

Temperance reminds us that life is the greatest experiment and the adventure comes in learning something new. In this process, one reaps the eternal treasure of golden wisdom.

Divination

In Temperance, you become the alchemist, representing the ability to transform aspects of your life that need to change. This will require patience, flexibility, and self-restraint. The old adage of "what does not bend, breaks" is applicable here. Temperance may be a time where it is necessary to modify your attitude. For example, if you are angry about something, try adopting a positive attitude. You may be surprised by how a change in perspective can work to transform a situation. This path often represents the desire to expand one's knowledge, especially that of a spiritual nature. By opening yourself to learning through experience, wisdom will come to you in many different forms.

XV—The Devil

Path of: Fear
Ruler: Capricorn

*What brings us out of comfort and fear is
imagination—creativity. Those who truly love danger
aren't extreme athletes, triathaloners or mountaineers.
Creative people plunge into disaster every time they
do something new; they risk everything that's familiar
to them.*

—John Tarrant

I n the previous Arcanum, Temperance, we met a present and forceful angel. In The Devil, we experience the angel's counterpart or shadow side. The Devil is one of the most difficult cards of the Tarot to interpret as its very presence carries many meanings and misperceptions. To fully understand this path, we must put aside superstitious images of black magic, witchcraft, and evil. Some would say there is no such thing as the devil, that it is a creation of the human imagination. In this card, The Devil is very real in the sense that it represents our inner most fears and unresolved desires. The Devil is a projection of our dark side.

We see The Devil in this card as a grotesque figure, a beast with bat wings. We first met the beast in the Strength card, representing our primal, animal nature. The Devil can represent procreative energy: the vital force fueling our sexual and creative power. Throughout time, the devil often appears as a serpent and there is usually a test accompanying his presence. Transmutation is much like a snake shedding its skin. Here we apply the art of alchemy (that is, the Temperance card), of transforming this vital energy into creative power. As in the Strength card, love is the key to a compassionate transformation.

Capricorn, an Earth sign and the sign of the goat, is the ruler of The Devil card. Representing the established order, this sign is by nature materialistic—the mountain goat with the endurance and fortitude to climb to the peaks of achievement. Often controlled, and concerned with appearance, it is the very measure of propriety. Yet Capricorn is also associated with the Greek deity Pan, the hoofed and horned god of the woodlands. Pan is a fertility god who played his magic flute and filled humans with fear, for he took away their strength by casting a spell of unrelenting lust and desire. The devil represents the earthiest component of human nature, the instincts of the body. This card signals a time where we may need to take a break from duty and responsibility: to release our inhibitions and experience our own personal Dionysian rites of divine decadence. The danger lies in going too far. Remember, by playing with fire sometimes one can get burned.

With The Devil we seek a balance between self-discipline and healthy escapism. This requires an attunement with our bodies.

When our needs and desires are repressed they can turn into projected judgment, looking for a scapegoat to blame for our unresolved issues. The darkest component of The Devil is a loss of faith in ourselves and in others.

The sign of Capricorn also represents power and ambition. This card exhibits the potential for power struggles. On The Devil's path, we discover whether or not we are manipulating others for our own means. The dark side of ambition is control, to get what we want at all costs, where negative materialism—the fear of not having—begins to rule our very thoughts and actions.

Mythology tells us that Lucifer (the devil) was an angel cast out of heaven for the sin of pride, or hubris. Interestingly, the original meaning of hubris is sexual passion. Lucifer is the light bringer, the dweller of the flame. If life is hell, then we are asked to consider the possibility that we have created it. On this path, we descend into the flames in order to transform our darkness into light.

A simple definition of this card is *burning through fear*. Like the Shamanic tradition of walking on hot coals, here we fire-walk and release our fears. Meeting our dark side can result in an inner power struggle between two aspects of self—the dark and the light. We can be found wrestling with inner demons and going "mad" in the process. The dark side can represent our secret self. Make friends with it because to ignore it will surely sabotage you.

This card shows a male and female in chains, in bondage to the devil. Yet if we look closely, we see that their chains are loose; they can choose to slip out of them. Here, we are offered the choice to release ourselves from the bonds that steal our power. A good sense of humor is helpful, as laughter can break spells. Your humor can give you the ability to take a step back and laugh at the cosmic joke.

Divination

An important distinction on this path is that you are not your fear. The fears you're experiencing are neon markers for the things you've been seeking to change, aspects of self that have been restricting your journey forward. Let go of such fear-based behaviors as obsession, addiction, and control. Also on the list is relinquishing judgment of self and others, thoughts like, "I'm not good enough," "he/she doesn't love me," and "I'll never have what I need." The substitution of material goods or gains to escape the journey is not your answer. Although it may feel harsh, facing your fears will transform you. Creative people take risks. Ultimately, the only thing you have to lose is your fear.

XVI—The Tower

Path of: Destruction
Ruler: Mars

*The elders have sent me here to tell you that now is
like a great, rushing river. And this will be experienced
in many different ways. There are those who would
hold onto the shore—there is no shore. The shore is
crumbling. Push off into the middle of the river.*

—Choquosh, Native American Storyteller

he Tower card presents a frightening picture. Here we see a towering fortress struck by a bolt of lightning and unwitting souls falling to their seeming demise in its fiery destruction. In some archaic decks, The Tower was called *The Lightning*, or "Le Feu du Ciel," meaning *Fire from Heaven*, bringing to mind images of biblical proportion—fire and brimstone, the punishing wrath of an angry, unsatisfied god.

Indeed, The Tower closely parallels the legendary story of "The Tower of Babel," a fable of humankind's attempt to conquer the heavens through a false system of values. The Tower of Babel symbolizes the sins of pride, conceit, and over-confidence.

What are we to make of such a card, and more importantly, its implications? First, we need a little perspective. Our world, the world we live in today, is in a sense a tower, meaning that the fundamental structures, the institutions (government, religion, law, and commerce) that humankind has created and accepted through decades and centuries of time are no longer working for us. Simply put, they have become obsolete. These decaying towers must be dismantled before a process of renewal and restoration can take place.

Gerd Ziegler, in his book *Tarot: Mirror of the Soul*, describes The Tower in this way: "Just as the extraction of a rotten tooth provides relief for the entire body, the destruction of stagnant situations and relations which hinder growth begins a healing process for your entire organism. Having a tooth extracted can be painful, but when the tooth is poisoning your system, there is no other choice."

A simple definition of this card is *fundamental change*. The Tower represents a test of what you value and hold to be true, what is essential to your growth and well-being. In a universal context, The Tower symbolizes the destruction of an old order so that a new order can arise. In the next Arcanum, The Star represents this prophesized new order: the manifestation of an era of enlightenment for all humanity.

On a personal level The Tower card represents a death, not in the physical sense, but in endings, extreme change, and ultimately transformation and rebirth. The Tower is external change, as compared with the Death card, which represents internal change. The Tower usually indicates an extreme shift in our outer reality, meaning the structures of our everyday life.

Mars, the fieriest of all planets (with the exception of the sun), rules The Tower. Fire represents the desire for growth, a force of energy that cannot be contained or denied. Mars is the God of War and Destruction, here signifying purification and cleansing by fire, a need for growth at all costs. By its very nature, destruction implies chaos, and on this path, we must be willing to embrace the concept of creative chaos. It is through chaos, no matter how uncomfortable or even painful, that creativity is born and new life comes into being.

The Tower card is often associated with the mythological bird the Phoenix, representing death and renewal. According to legend, when the Phoenix saw death draw near, it would make a nest of sweet-smelling wood and resins, then expose itself to the full force of the sun's rays until it burst into flames. Another Phoenix would then arise from its ashes. This path represents the necessity of periodic destruction in our lives so that recreation and regeneration can ultimately take place.

Divination

You are experiencing an extreme cycle of change requiring you to let go of old structures in your life that no longer serve you. Do not try to control or manipulate this change. Instead, trust that by letting go of the old, a new sense of order will arise. You will find it easier to go with the flow. This could be an unsettling time and you may feel like you have nothing to hold onto. Still, you must let go. When overwhelmed, pray for grace. During this period, you may experience sudden flashes of insight or perception, like a flash of lightning in a thunderstorm, clarity with glimpses of what is to come. This is not the moment for rebuilding. Rebuilding will come later. For now, cry the tears of the Phoenix and heal your wounds. This healing is an important part of the process, of you making way for the new.

XVII—The Star

Path of: Inspiration
Ruler: Aquarius

Gather out of star-dust
Earth-dust, Cloud-dust, Storm-dust
And splinters of hail,
One handful of dream-dust
Not for sale.

—Langston Hughes

From the ruins of The Tower appears The Star, a bright and welcome light. It is no coincidence that The Star follows in The Tower's destructive wake. Through the path of The Tower, our structures and foundations were torn asunder. This restructuring occurs because the immense creative potential of The Star could never be contained within The Tower's restrictive walls. It is only *after* the tearing away of past limitations that The Star is free to shine. Here, the Phoenix rises from the ashes.

Aquarius rules The Star. The symbol for Aquarius is the "water-bearer," which may be confusing, as Aquarius is an Air sign. To understand, we must take the concept of Air and expand it beyond the mundane, from the realm of the mind and the intellect into a larger sphere, through the ethers and into the realm of energy and space. Aquarius is the vessel for cosmic energy, the universal waters of consciousness, and what is sometimes referred to as the Universal or Cosmic Mind. Through The Star, we connect to the unlimited destiny of all humankind.

The woman pictured here is the goddess Nuith, Our Lady of the Stars. She holds two cups (or chalices), symbolizing the merging of two streams of consciousness: the Greater Conscious into the Individual Conscious. She pours the heavenly waters into the earth. The Star is a channel symbolizing the ancient and sacred treatise, "as above, so below." This path represents heaven on earth; it is the manifestation of the celestial into material form.

The Star is the first of the three "Luminaries" of the Tarot deck (followed by The Moon and The Sun). A Luminary is a source of light. The Star is *creative light*, or inspiration. One definition of inspiration is, "the act of drawing breath into the body." Inspiration is divine breath, the taking in of divinity and the receiving of spirit. Creativity is a gift from God and it comes from spirit. You, as the artist, in whatever form this may take, are a channel for this divine force. The artist and poet William Blake described this creative power as the imagination and said it was God itself.

A simple definition of this card is *the power of dreams.* Dreams and imagination are essential to the future of humankind. For without our innate ability to imagine, to dream, to be that small hopeful child who wishes upon a star, we would be lost to a world of the ordinary and the mundane. Through our creative mind, we become poet, artist, leader, and visionary. We are immortal, magical, and we can touch the stars.

The Star is the most encompassing card of the deck in the sense that it inspires us to cultivate largesse of spirit. The power of The Star lies in its ability to inspire greatness, not only in us, but in others as well. The Star represents creative brilliance, the ego and the personality elevated. Stars are generous with their light. They are leaders and motivators. This path encourages us to transcend our limitations and to connect to a higher purpose and vision, not only for our own sake, but ultimately, for the sake of all humanity.

Within us all lies The Star's potential. Yet manifesting one's dreams requires a great deal of faith. The Star card is often associated with the "Star of Bethlehem," symbolizing the recognition of cosmic forces greater than ourselves. These forces lead us to an unknown destiny. They also remind us of The Hermit's journey and his test of faith. With The Star, like The Hermit, we must believe enough in our power and our vision to chance the unknown and see where it will take us.

In Kabalistic teachings, The Star is represented by the letter Tzaddi, meaning "fish hook." Here lies a poetic idea, that it is time to cast your line out into the great sea of imagination and see what you will catch. A fly-fisher would describe their process as both an art and a meditation. Remember, if you don't like your catch, you can always throw it back into the ocean.

Divination

You are creating your future now. This is a time for expanding your vision, for opening yourself to a whole new realm of possibilities. Think big! You are only limited by the bounds of your imagination. What inspires you? What is your dearest wish, your dream? Greatness comes from your faith to believe, especially in yourself. Trust your vision even if you are not sure where it will take you, or of its exact form. Be willing to experiment with all possibilities. Don't worry if others don't understand; you may be ahead of your time. Radiate confidence. Think of yourself as a pioneer, a shining light for others to follow. This could prove to be an exceptionally creative period for you. Dance fearlessly with your muses and let them guide you to manifesting what can be.

XVIII—The Moon

Path of: Darkness
Ruler: Pisces

A promise to control the tide is always a lie. The resolute moon is more persistent than the best of intentions.

—Claudia Mauro

e enter into uncharted territory through the 18th Arcanum—The Moon. These are the dark and murky waters of the subconscious, the subterranean depths of mind and soul. The Moon card is associated with what has been known to mystics for centuries as the dark night of the soul. The Moon's dark journey is one that is not always willingly taken, for at times it can be both frightening and disorienting. The Bogeyman comes in the night, and on this path we dance with inner demons and ghosts from the past. Yet for better or for worse, in darkness, we have no choice but to merge with our shadow.

The Moon card looks both sinister and alluring. Here we see a full moon ripe with secrets. Two watchtowers stand beneath it. The towers guard the threshold to an invisible world, the dark void of the unknown. On this card, a wolf and a dog are seen baying at the moon. The use of the number two is significant as it represents the dual nature of this card and reminds us of the Tarot's second Arcanum, The High Priestess and the Queen of the Moon. Moonlight can be deceptive, casting an illusory light. Here we may feel caught between two worlds, the real and the unreal.

The wolf and the dog are two aspects of The Moon. The wolf is a totem for our most basic animal instincts, representing primal psychic energy. The dog is Anubis, the Egyptian god of the underworld, and here truly man's best friend. Anubis guides lost souls through the many hidden dangers of the underworld. His presence on this card sends the important message that we do not have to be alone in this journey. We can seek help and guidance in negotiating the darkness.

Finally we see a crayfish, representing Cancer, the astrological ruler of the moon (or a dung-beetle, the Egyptian scarab that carries the sun across the horizon). The crayfish is shown rising out of a muddy pool. The pool represents unconscious waters that may have become stagnant and lifeless. The result can be an emotional stagnation, a feeling of being stuck in the deep muck of one's past. This may lead to depression and profound despair, yet there is cause for hope. In some interpretations, the crayfish is actually a scorpion, representing Scorpio (the astrological sign of death and rebirth) and symbolizing emotional and spiritual regeneration. This signals that it is time to emerge from the depths of darkness and reach for the light. A simple definition of this card is *a soul in search of rebirth.*

The Moon is the second of the Tarot's Luminaries or "lights." It is the very act of opening ourselves to the light, as we did in "The Star," that attracts the dark. The brighter the light, the more our darkness becomes apparent. The Moon is Reflected Light, mirroring the light of the sun. The goal in this card is to go from the dark side of the moon, a place that no light can reach, to a place of reflection, which leads to illumination. Ultimately, The Moon represents the journey of enlightenment.

Pisces rules The Moon, symbolized as two fish swimming in opposite directions, and again representing a conflict between two worlds, or two realities. Pisces are sensitive creatures, greatly open to the non-physical psychic realm. Those with strong moon characteristics have a highly developed feminine nature representing the intuitive, feeling, and receptive aspects of self. This combination makes one highly attuned to unseen influences, especially the influence of other people: their emotions, needs, and projections. On this path, we must be careful not to be pulled into other people's "stuff." The Moon suggests a time for setting clear boundaries, for separating our needs from the needs of others.

This realm is a tricky one, for moonlight is always elusive and cannot be caught. Nonetheless, we must be willing to delve into the inner mystery, facing phantasms along the way. It is an understatement to say that this card offers profound wisdom, a wisdom that can only come from darkness. In the process of seeking and attaining wisdom, The Moon can be a most powerful ally.

Divination

If you have chosen this card, it is time for an emotional house cleaning to clear out the cobwebs of the past, to bring to closure parts of your life that are holding you back. This may require going outside of your comfort zone as you let go of old behaviors or relationships that no longer serve you. It is easy to be caught in The Moon's spell, so here we must be careful not to become enamored or bewitched by our illusions. Spend time with your dreamscape; in that realm you will reacquaint yourself with your deepest nature. To explore the gifts of your darkness, you may need to enter a period of hibernation. It is always darkest before the light.

XIX—The Sun

Path of: Joy
Ruler: The Sun

*Give forth thy light to all without doubt; the clouds
and shadows are no matter for thee.*

—Aleister Crowley

he Sun itself is the planetary ruler of this card. This is the first indication of the beautiful simplicity inherent to this path. The Sun card encourages us to look at the world through the eyes of a child, with purity and simplicity, without forethought to agendas or worry of outcomes. Gazing upon the bright imagery of this card, one cannot help but feel a sense of optimism and joy. Just as the sun rises in the east and sets in the west, with each new morning, with each light of day, we experience an awakening—a rebirth. In The Moon, we encountered the dark and sleepy illusions of night. In The Sun, we experience the clarity that comes from one who has been reborn. The Sun symbolizes the beginning of a brand-new day.

The sun is the center of our solar system, and all planets orbit around it. It is our brightest and fieriest star. Through The Sun card, we connect to the need to shine, the desire to be seen and to express one's own unique self, one's own light. The sun is a symbol for our life force—the divine spark of self—our true essence. In astrology, the sun represents the light of the personality, which is in a state of constant evolution as we experience life. The personality, with all of its unique and colorful nuances, is the vehicle for the expression of one's self in this lifetime. The anchor for self is the ego. Often the ego gets a bad rap, seen as vain or selfish. Yet, without your ego, there would be no focus for the light.

The sun is dynamic and magnetic, a powerful source. It is no wonder then that since antiquity the sun has been worshipped as a supreme deity representing great power and strength. The astrological symbol for the sun is a circle with a dot in the middle, ultimately representing wholeness. When self-expression comes from a place of centered-ness and well-being, it is a truly magnificent sight to behold. It becomes sheer joy—the freedom and exhilaration of expressing one's self. A simple definition of this card is *enthusiasm*.

The Sun completes the trinity of the Tarot's Luminaries, representing Revealed Light. The Sun presents freedom. This is a freedom from not only one's personal and emotional past (The Moon), but also on a deeper level from past karmic cycles. In the highest sense, there is no "baggage" on this path. The result is that here we have nothing to hide. The Sun offers the freedom to reveal ourselves, to share our light without concern about what others may think or how we will be received, what could be described as a release of all expectation. Robert Wang, in *The Qabalistic Tarot*, describes The Sun as a *new innocence*. He writes, "It is, quite literally, a growing younger, a process of birth backwards until we reach a stage where there is some recollection of the source from which we emerged."

The energy of The Sun is transformative. In alchemy, the sun (or sulfur) is an important ingredient in the symbolic process of transforming lead into gold. The heat of the sun ignites within us a positive force, a purifying influence that can turn the most base of matter into something precious and beautiful. Through this path, we experience the "golden touch" in all endeavors, hence The Sun's traditional definition: *success!*

If there is a challenge in The Sun, then it is a happy one: adjusting to enjoyment and taking pleasure in your newfound success. We live in a complicated world and today's society has become acclimated to an unhealthy diet of worry and stress. It is easy to get caught up in all the hustle and bustle of life, the pressure to be busy, hurry, get ahead, and solve all your problems. The message of The Sun is simple: *Don't worry, be happy.*

Divination

Here are seven steps to embracing the successful essence of The Sun.

1. Live your life in the present.

2. Experience each moment fully. Look around you to see and feel the wonders of all creation.

3. Pretend that you do not have a care or worry in the world.

4. Be like a child whose only agenda is to simply be, to play and frolic in the light of the sun.

5. When experiencing a problem or dilemma trust that by letting go, it will be resolved in a beneficial way.

6. Be active. Whenever possible, say yes. Why? Because you can.

7. Then, and most importantly, become the light and shine your magnificent presence unto the world. Your mantra now: everyday, in every way, my life gets better and better.

XX—Judgment

Path of: Reckoning
Ruler: Pluto
Element: Fire

Prayer is an egg.
Hatch out
the total helplessness
inside.

—Rumi

he image portrayed in this card is of the biblical "Last Judgment," also known as the Day of Reckoning. By definition, reckoning means to deal with, the settlement of accounts. Simply stated, it is accountability. There comes a moment in life where one is forced to look into the harsh mirror of reality, where illusion and pretension are stripped away and one comes face to face with what is the true self. This moment is the essence of the Judgment card. This is the end of your world, or at least some part of it, as you currently know it.

Yet, the Judgment card is not a death sentence, although in the moment it may very well seem that way. In fact, this card represents just the opposite. Through the path of Judgment, there is opportunity. There is the potential for a renewal, an awakening of such magnitude that it may be overwhelming to comprehend and, in the beginning, difficult to incorporate. But before we deal with the rebirth inherent to this card, we must first address the death.

The ruler for the Judgment card is Pluto. In astrology, this planet symbolizes death and rebirth. On a mundane level, this means change and growth. On a higher level, Pluto is the soul in its experience of transformation. Transformation can sometimes be painful, for it is often stimulated by crisis. Without the crisis, we would not be forced to deal with the changes that are necessary to our growth. Pluto is truth, in the sense of a naked soul stripped to its very essence, an experience that could be described as "meeting your maker" totally exposed.

The element for Judgment is Fire. Fire is the creative life force; it is the purest expression of free will. Fire is inherently growth-oriented and it can be intense in its desire for change. The element of Fire can have a purifying effect, burning away the past to give rise to the future. In Judgment, it represents a baptism by fire. This path lets you choose between rebirth and death, Heaven and Hell. It asks, "If you were to die today, what would be your regrets? Did you walk your talk? Did you speak your truth?" These are intimidating questions, questions that boil down to personal integrity.

Don't panic. Notice the angel so magnificently pictured here. He is the Archangel Michael, the leader of the forces of light and the sun, symbolizing rebirth. It is said that Michael routed the devil and hosts of darkness in the war of Heaven. He blows a trumpet, calling souls to rebirth. Richard Cavendish, in his book on the Tarot, quotes Michael's message as, "We can rise from the grave of our old dead self now, while we are still in the physical body, if our ears are not deaf to the trumpet call from on high."

To quote the Buddha, "There is only one time when it is essential to awaken. That time is now." The Judgment card is a call to action. It is never too late to make change, and now more than ever. This card represents a turning point in consciousness; a point where personal will aligns with the higher soul in a quest for truth. A simple definition of this card is *conscious rebirth.* The result is a more profound and honest reality.

The Judgment card requires a critical analysis of your life, a facing of facts. In this process, it is easy to get caught up in black and white thinking—good vs. bad. But on a higher level, there is no such thing as right or wrong. Essentially the whole point of "Judgment" is to not judge. Your life and your processes are between you and your God, or higher self, and the same goes for others. The purpose here is not to condemn, but to inspire one to make changes for a higher good. Ultimately in the Judgment, severity is subdued, giving way to hope and to mercy. On this path, we are encouraged toward tolerance, not only for ourselves, but also for those around us. It is said that unless you have walked in someone else's shoes, you cannot truly understand their journey. In honoring your own choices, you can then honor the choices of others.

Divination

The Judgment card represents a wake-up call, a time to commune with your higher self. Now is the moment for a reassessment of your life. To make amends and bring into settlement any old or unresolved issues, accounts, or relationships. Your newfound consciousness is not an excuse to judge yourself. Remember, hindsight is always 20/20. Instead, congratulate yourself on your willingness to see your life from a more universal perspective. By taking care of outstanding matters, you will be free to experience your world in a way that is nothing short of rejuvenating. You are never helpless if you have the ability to change. Finally, at the end of the day, ask yourself: "Did I do the best that I could today?" If the answer is yes, then sing a triumphant Hallelujah, thank the powers that be, and be at peace with yourself—truly at peace.

XXI—The World

Path of: Wholeness
Ruler: Saturn

*Honor the past as your teacher, honor the present as
your creation, and honor the future as your
inspiration.*

—Crow, *Medicine Cards*

he World card represents the completion of our journey through the Tarot deck. This card is a synthesis of all paths before it, representing the accumulation of all the lessons that we have learned along the way. Now we must leave home and our inner exploration and venture into the outer world of form. Take all that we know and translate it into actual experience. When we get to The World, we have attained the wisdom and the tools necessary to create a reality that reflects our highest and truest selves. Here, the ever-evolving dream of all that we can be is finally within our grasp.

The ruler of The World card is Saturn. In astrology, this planet denotes boundaries and structure. On a physical level, it is the body, most specifically the skeletal structure, the inner foundation that shapes and defines our outer physical form. On a spiritual level Saturn symbolizes the earth's learning ground, the school of the soul. Saturn can be a hard taskmaster, for it teaches us our limitations. In ancient times, Saturn was Cronos, Father Time, representing our limited time on earth. In The World, we gain clarity about what we want to achieve in this time, defining our purpose in life. The World is the outer manifestation of this intention, relating to our career. We create an identity that others can recognize, and hopefully respect. On this path, we build our body of work in the world.

A simple definition of this card is *worldly success*. Experience the success that you have earned—that you deserve. Ultimately, The World represents the ability to be confident and proud of our accomplishments, but not arrogant. As we express our unique potential, the gifts that we were born with, we can inspire others to claim their own unique talents and abilities.

In the first Arcanum, The Magician, we realized the power of creative free will. The World is a mastery of the creative process of manifestation. Here we step into reality and realize that the life we experience is, for the most part, our own creation. In a sense, we grow up and become adults. We become empowered by embracing responsibility for creating the world that we live in. This encompasses our worlds, big and small, personal and universal. It is the balance of a bigger consciousness, the divine plan with individual free will.

The World is a completion, yet we still have much to learn. Here we have a sense of our destiny, but its full meaning has yet to unfold.

Now we can only discover its meaning by experiencing ourselves in the world. This will be a process of being separate and self-sufficient, yet at the same time a part of a whole picture.

The World card shows what looks to be a female dancer balancing in the center of the world. In older decks, the figure is actually a hermaphrodite, representing male and female qualities in perfect balance. The World symbolizes what the mystics describe as the alchemical marriage or union of male and female energy, the exquisite dance of Yin and Yang that leads us into an energetic wholeness.

We, as physical beings, are made of energy. This energy is regulated by the life force, the organic substance that defines matter. This life force evolves as we move through time, our very movements activating an energy field that creates the atmosphere. The World asks us to look at the energy that we send out into the universe. The rule of "like attracts like" is important here: Whatever you put out will come back to you. In a positive sense, The World is coming into harmony with the earth flow.

The World card is a process of redefining our boundaries, a time where we expand our current structures to encompass a more worldly view. On a mundane level, this may translate to travel, to exploring the world at large. Here we become citizens of the world with the desire to pass on what we know and participate in a larger global consciousness.

Divination

Now is a time to take all that you have learned into the world. You have just graduated from the School of Life. Confidence is your calling card, so don't be shy about celebrating your accomplishments. This is not showing off, but announcing your presence to the world in a positive way. You deserve acknowledgement. This card represents expansion and new opportunities, especially in regards to your career. The world is your oyster, but you are asked to take responsibility for what happens next. It is up to you. This is a time to step up to the plate and go to bat for what you believe. You are in a dance of creation and manifestation. Be clear about the energy you send out, because it will define the measure of success that you receive.

6

MODERN REFLECTIONS

o—The Fool

here are many fools in history. These are unique individuals who take a bold stance against the hierarchy, revolutionaries and rule-breakers who take pleasure in defying the established order. Aleister Crowley was very much a fool. He was infamous, controversial, undeniably brilliant, and ahead of his time. Crowley was a British mystic who began to make a name for himself at the turn of the 19th century—the fin de siècle—a time when magic and mysticism were becoming vogue in many social circles. Crowley was a Magus of the highest order of the Golden Dawn, a Hermetic brotherhood dedicated to a scholarly exploration of magic, the Kabbalah, and the Tarot.

Crowley's *The Book of Thoth (The Egyptian Tarot)* has been scoured and studied, earmarked and underlined, by many a devotee of the Tarot. I bought my first copy of *The Book of Thoth* at a second-hand bookstore. There were so many notations in the margins that I eventually gave up and bought a new copy.

Crowley was obsessed with the Tarot. You could say that he was high on knowledge. In reading his works, one can almost become intoxicated. You will feel his influence here in this book.

Crowley's deck, The Thoth Tarot, is one of most popular Tarot decks in use today. Yet at the time of its introduction, it was groundbreaking. The illustrations by Lady Frieda Harris are avant-garde and vaguely cubist in appearance. This was a time when most Tarot decks were either based on ancient imagery or looked positively medieval. Crowley's deck was not published until after his death. He did not live to see his greatest work acknowledged. Crowley was ahead of his time—the mark of a fool. His work is timeless and still of relevance today.

Crowley was notorious because he was a hedonist and an egomaniac. He also flirted with devil worship. Eventually, later in life, Crowley

THE FOOL.

succumbed to an opium addiction. He represents a cautionary tale of a fool—the precarious line between exploration and sheer outrageousness. Crowley defied the sanctity of the Golden Dawn, forsaking his vows to the order as he exposed the secrets of their work to the general public. Aleister Crowley liberated knowledge. He was a mystic revolutionary. Ultimately, Crowley was expelled from the order, with much drama. Was he insane or inspired? Perhaps both.

Fools have always been prevalent in the arts, in today's music industry in particular. The musician and rock star Mick Jagger, of Rolling Stones fame, is a modern-day fool. Jagger could be described as trickster incarnate. Many acknowledge him as a musical maverick, brilliant and controversial. Jagger presents a puckish figure, androgynous and totally outrageous in his creative expression. He helped to revolutionize the music scene in the 1960s, defying the establishment and ushering in a whole new era in music. Because the Rolling Stones were so blatantly sexual, even devilish, and were against old ways of music, they have in their time generated a lot of heat, especially from the conservative old guard.

Jagger can still strut his stuff. Even though he is well into middle age, he never seems to grow old. He is still active and vital. Fools can sometimes be Peter Pans, not wanting to grow up. They can embody the characteristics of old and young. They are, in a sense, timeless. It would be an understatement to say that Jagger's work with the Rolling Stones liberated music, introducing rock and roll to the mainstream. Their albums have sold millions of copies.

Jagger's defiant and indifferent stance towards the media and his critics, not to mention his reputation as a playboy, has been another source of trouble. Is he playing against politics or just crazy like a fox? Let us not forget that Mick Jagger is currently one of the richest men in the world. Fools are often ridiculed, even crucified, for their talents or beliefs, but ultimately prove to be catalysts for new ways of thinking.

Musician, rock star, author, and actress Madonna is a female version of The Fool, especially The Fool as shape-shifter. As we all know, Madonna loves to constantly reinvent herself. Fools can be chameleon-like, able to shift personas according to whim. Madonna is all about pushing buttons, especially regarding our religious and sexual beliefs. Like Mick Jagger, she has been fearless in acting on her inspiration. Whether you like her work or not, she has been a constant zeitgeist of the times.

In music today, rap artists are perhaps the new fools. There are many purists who vocally claim that rap music is not *real* music. The controversial rap-star Marshal Mathers (aka Eminem) is an extreme example of The Fool as a rule-breaker and provocateur. Fiercely passionate, and with a criminal rap sheet, Eminem has been hugely popular with a youthful audience looking for new paths to self-expression. He has blatantly defied societal beliefs regarding sex, violence, and drugs. Eminem is a Wild Card, often taking on the persona of The Joker. He is much like a court jester, defying the Kings and Queens of the music industry, yet he is just brilliant and comical enough to get our attention.

The archetype of the fool shows up in folklore and literature as well. Take for example in Cervantes' *Don Quixote,* "El Loco" is known as the errant knight chasing windmills and pursuing a dream of love. Or consider Robin Hood and his band of Merry Men, stealing from the rich and giving to the poor. And in fairy tales there is the story of the disguised wandering prince, or better yet the witch disguised as a beggar who grants three wishes to the man who offers her help. They all repeat the themes of The Fool as dreamer, trickster, and master of disguise.

Gerald's story is a modern day Fool tale. Gerald was leaving a social event in a questionable neighborhood and was feeling a bit nervous and on guard. As Gerald was making his way to his car, a street person—disheveled in appearance and seemingly a bit crazy— approached him. Gerald assumed that this person would ask him for money. Instead he simply said to Gerald, "You look smart. Don't worry." Then he walked away.

Some background is in order to understand the full weight of this encounter. Gerald is an attorney and at the time of this story, was in a major life transition. He was leaving a secure legal practice to explore other options. He was also on the verge of bankruptcy. Gerald was feeling very much like a fool on the edge of a precipice, about to jump into a totally unknown future. On this particular night he was ruminating on these changes and how foolish they might be. He was especially worried about what his peers thought about him. The stranger had delivered the very words Gerald needed to hear—that he was capable enough to figure things out and that he would be okay during his transition. Was this confirmation from a higher plane? You decide.

When Gerald recovered from his shock, the mysterious stranger was nowhere to be seen. Gerald even wondered if he had imagined him. Perhaps you have had a similar experience of receiving acknowledgment from an unknown source or a stranger just when you needed it most. This would be The Fool at work. The Fool says to expect the unexpected, that miracles come in many packages and many personas.

Fools always evoke strong reactions. But we need our fools: brave souls daring enough to walk fine lines, to challenge the established order, and most importantly to fearlessly act on their inspiration. That is perhaps why God looks so kindly toward them and, ultimately, why the world embraces them.

The Fool can apply to different situations in your life. Because he is a shape shifter, The Fool may have different meanings and applications. For example, The Fool is unreliable in all relationship situations (think Mick Jagger), often not wanting the responsibility or commitment that a relationship entails. In regards to work, The Fool could mean a restless time, a time where you are straining at the leash, ready to take a chance or risk regarding your career. When The Fool shows up in your reading, he represents unexpected outcomes in the situation.

I—The Magician

hen we think about a magician today, images of rabbits pulled from hats, sleight of hand, and card tricks may come to mind. Las Vegas style illusions of disappearing acts, and lovely ladies sawed in half that are the fortes of entertainers and magicians such as Penn and Teller or David Copperfield may also come up. There is also David Blaine, the young, brash, and controversial magician who has staged feats of endurance in the name of magic. But it is Harry Houdini whose name is most synonymous with modern magic. He is perhaps the most famous magician of our time. Houdini was greatly interested in the occult and his death itself is still shrouded in mystery. Houdini's most famous trick was to wrap his body in chains and submerge himself in a tank of water. In these moments we were suspended in time and reality, wondering if he would be able to free himself.

What all these magicians might share with you if asked is that their art is an illusion: a process of tricking the mind. They would

also remind you that there is an element of danger to all these acts. Most important to The Magician's path, they would say that their magic takes a lot of work and practice to make it seem real.

Before magic became entertainment, it was an ancient art practiced since the beginning of time. Magic is the manifestation of intent, a process of the will directed. It requires concentration and discipline. The formula for this card is simple and is one known and exercised by magicians through time, "The Magician's hocus pocus is his ability to focus."

THE MAGICIAN.

One of my clients, a shaman well-versed in the ancient art of magic, once shared with me a traditional magician's discipline or "trick." In the process of creating something new in your life, concentrate on the desired manifestation or happening, then send it out into the universe. The secret, she said, was that then you had to let it go. If you kept thinking about it, you interfered with its ability to manifest. This illustrates the timeless concept of not sharing your wish with others because it takes away from (or loses) its power. Another method in the process of creation is the ancient magician's talent for invoking through the power of words. Affirmations are one example of this concept.

To explore your inner magician and your power of the mind to create, try this exercise. Imagine a blank frame with no picture and then fill it with what you want to have happen. Put the image into a balloon, release it into the universe, and go about your business. You might be surprised how often you receive your wish. If it doesn't happen don't be discouraged; consider the possibility that it is not in alignment with your higher good.

The Magician card asserts that manifestation is 10 percent inspiration and 90 percent perspiration. Athletes know this well. Just watch the grace and elegance of Olympian ice skaters. They make it look simple, but it comes from years of practice. Dick Buttons, a former ice skater and television commentator, once remarked that the difference between an athlete and a champion is discipline. When asked what the winning formula was, he said simply, "Practice, practice, practice."

There are many contemporary writings on the subject of mind over matter. Shakti Gawain, in her pioneering book *Creative Visualization*, is a noteworthy example. *The Nature of Personal Reality*, by Jane Roberts, was my first and most profound encounter with the idea that our minds form our very reality and existence. Most recently, Eckhart Tolle's bestselling *The Power of Now* speaks to the power of the mind and how it can deceive. These are modern "magician's books," translating ancient concepts into our times and providing us with knowledge that empowers our ability to create our reality.

The Magician's dark side is sometimes called black magic. When out of balance, it can represent the use of power to manipulate and intimidate others. The story of Matt and Cynthia is a perfect example of how this can occur. This couple was struggling to make a new business enterprise work, but they felt plagued by misfortune.

In the past, Matt and Cynthia had been involved in a spiritual group who practiced magic. Their teacher was a charismatic figure that held power over the group. They became uncomfortable with his practices, especially his guru-like influence. Disillusioned, they decided to leave.

Problems began to arise with their business, and they became worried that their teacher had put a hex on them. In their reading, The Magician card reminded them that they were creating their own reality. They were making the hex real because they believed in it. We discussed that no one can put a curse on you unless you believe they can. The same goes for most superstitious beliefs. For example, if you break a mirror, you will have seven years of bad luck. Or if you walk under a ladder, you will have personal misfortune. These ideas are mind tricks that take away from our personal power and our ability to create what we wish to experience.

Matt and Cynthia have made a conscious choice to not experience any "black magic." This empowers them to make necessary changes in their business without the veil of fear. The realization that their experience was of their own creation was not only liberating, but also beneficial to their bank account.

In this card, we become aware that magic is a form of personal power. The sign of infinity, a figure eight turned on its side, hovers over The Magician's head. It represents his timeless connection to all possibilities. In his hand he holds a magic wand, representing his gift to manifest. In the highest sense, The Magician represents an alignment with a greater purpose, meaning that your magic can serve both yourself and others.

Another example of The Magician card is Sunyi's story. An attorney by profession, and also a budding writer, Sunyi had recently signed with a publishing house, and she was very excited. This put her in the position of finishing her book while at the same time keeping up her law practice. Sunyi could be described as the responsible type, and she herself would tell you that she is the classic "Type A" personality. This served her well in her law practice and her clients were grateful because she went the extra mile for them.

When Sunyi came for her reading, she was extremely stressed out because she had to juggle a lot of balls in the air, like The Magician (the juggler). In trying to be everything to everyone, she felt like was losing her self. She did not have enough time for herself, let alone her writing process. Sunyi is a Buddhist, and she noted that her practice of meditation was very helpful to her, connecting her to the ability to be present in the moment. This helped her to feel sane and in charge, even during the most difficult of moments. During this time her attention to mindfulness allowed her to focus on the tasks at hand without distraction, in a sense, to be free from time.

Writing was a whole new world for Sunyi. Here she was not an expert, as she was in the arena of law. The book represented a new beginning, and she had to be willing to learn something new again. The Zen phrase that was especially powerful to her (you could say it became her affirmation) was, "In the beginner's mind there are many possibilities, in the expert's mind there are few."

When The Magician shows up in your reading, it represents a time where you may be learning and in the process of developing your talents and abilities in a whole new way. In application, this means the willingness to make mistakes. The Magician often represents the beginning of a new business enterprise. Whether in business affairs or relationships, here we are students.

My personal experience with this card is that it usually denotes those with a gift for communication. The Magician's ruler, Mercury, represents communication. This may be oral or in writing. This card frequently comes up for those with artistic natures, creative types, who are not necessarily in a creative profession. To me, The Magician often represents writers, whether they are aware of their ability or not. Sometimes they may see it as an unfulfilled wish. The Magician card could be an affirmation to you that you do indeed have a gift for writing and, if you have not already, it is the time to explore this talent.

II—The High Priestess

The High Priestess reminds us that there is nothing new under the sun. The story behind this card is a timeless and universal scenario, perhaps as old as the moon itself. To put it bluntly, it is the story of a woman misunderstood. The High Priestess is ruled by the moon, which is a universal symbol for the feminine. Women are lunar creatures. In a spiritual sense, the feminine is sacred, representing the very mystery of life. On a physical level the feminine is the sacred vessel of life, representing a woman's ability to give birth.

The High Priestess is our connection to the sacred feminine in terms of knowledge. She represents what is often referred to as women's knowing, intuition, or sometimes a woman's hypersensitivity. Technically, it is the sixth sense—our psychic perception.

Psychic comes from the Greek word psyche, meaning soul. We are all psychic, including men. Many times when I broach the subject with clients who are starting to experience this ability, their

THE HIGH PRIESTESS

reaction is a mixture of awe and dread. "Me, psychic? No way!" Maybe the client had a negative psychic experience or was raised to believe that psychic activities are somehow evil, like witches, werewolves, and devil-worshippers. In my work, I have often found that clients associate the word with images of a 1-800-Psychic Network with Madame Whoever's supposed direct line to their future. For many people, the word psychic is scary and can be a real button-pusher. It may represent a dark and unknown force, or something unnatural. Darkness and the unknown are both words associated with the moon and the symbolic feminine.

If I use the term intuition when referring to this same sense, it is usually acknowledged, sometimes grudgingly. "Yes, I guess I'm intuitive." Intuition is a faculty of the psychic process. By definition, it means "a direct perception of truth or fact independent of any reasoning process, a keen and quick insight." For many, the word intuition is more safe and comfortable than the word psychic. The term psychic has been greatly misunderstood and maligned, carrying centuries of superstition. Psychic means "of the human soul" and is a natural human ability; it is particularly sensitive to the influence of nonphysical forces.

Our gift of intuition or psychic ability comes in many forms. Perhaps you have heard the term clairvoyant (which merely means "to see clearly"), psycho kinesis, telepathic, or medium. These are all psychic abilities/terms. The movie *The Sixth Sense,* where the little boy says he "sees dead people," is a graphic example of psychic phenomenon. For most, experiencing psychic ability or intuition is not quite so dramatic as in film. Usually it is more subtle, a sense of knowing or realization. On this path, we explore our psychic and intuitive abilities, which work differently for everyone.

There was time in our world when the Goddess was worshipped as the source of all-being, a time where the calendar was based not on the sun, but on the many cycles of the moon. This was the zenith of The High Priestess. Many spiritualists say that the Goddess is now experiencing a revival, that we are entering into a period of time where there will be a renaissance of the feminine energy. This is not the appropriate place for a political or religious discussion on the topic, but books such as *The DaVinci Code* by Dan Brown explore this idea further. Brown reminds us that the Goddess is everywhere around us, especially apparent in our relationships with symbols. People connected to The High Priestess often have a tremendous affinity for the Goddess. She may have gone underground as Brown says, into the shadows and a secret life, but then the moon is the most powerful in darkness.

For some, The High Priestess is like a dusty portrait, a part of self that has been forgotten or mislaid. For others, it is a mirror that we look in everyday. The High Priestess represents the sacred feminine—what could be described as one's infinite wisdom. If she shows up in your readings, meditations, or dreams, it could represent a part of yourself that needs to be healed or requires your attention.

The High Priestess type of person is quite prevalent in my clientele, among both men and women. Basically, they are individuals looking for recognition of their souls. They may come looking for a fortune-telling experience: "Tell me my future." I believe what they are really seeking is a form of spiritual sanctuary, a safe place to explore their deeper selves. In modern times, there are not many places where one can explore this aspect of self. If one is connected to a religion, perhaps it can be fulfilled in church, but spirituality and religion do not always align. People often seek out healers, counselors, or spiritualists to fulfill this need.

Here are two stories of different expressions of The High Priestess. The first is Ellen, an extremely psychic High Priestess, although she didn't realize it until we worked together. When pressed, Ellen explained with some embarrassment that she had experienced premonitions and psychic phenomena. She thought she was just a little crazy, so she ignored and repressed her psychic senses.

Ellen is middle-aged, mild-mannered, tentative, a bit shy, and easily overwhelmed. For example, directing her to my office, which is easy for most, was quite a process. Ellen had trouble in life dealing with the "real" world and the material plane, most specifically with money matters.

Ellen felt herself drawn to the mystery arts and was taking classes in everything: astrology, Reiki, soul retrieval, and past-ife regression. To put it mildly, she was on overload. She was also going from one psychic reader to another trying to gain clarity and find answers. The end result was that she was feeling extremely confused by all the information she was receiving from so many sources. Ellen was turning her power over to her teachers and readers, trusting them instead of herself.

We decided that Ellen should spend more time focusing on her inner journey, taking time to look within, to meditate for her own answers. This would put her more in touch with her own spiritual process as a way of developing and understanding her abilities. We also decided she should take a break from her esoteric studies and instead take a few classes in money management and finance to help her feel more functional in the world. As I followed her progress, I noted that Ellen was more grounded and willing to deal with her tangible needs.

Another story concerns Debbie, who, at the time of her reading, was an angry High Priestess. Debbie had worked in the business world most of her adult life, but always as an assistant or helper to those in power. Yet she is extremely powerful herself. She was "the power behind the throne" and was not happy about it. Debbie said that people in her workplace were constantly seeking her out for advice, insight, and wisdom, then resenting her later. It appears that sometimes one can know too much. There were repercussions for her knowledge, especially with regard to being the keeper of other people's secrets— a tricky business indeed.

Debbie is a catalyst, meaning that she puts people in touch with their deeper selves. The downside to this is that they don't always like it. She was feeling drained because she was getting too involved with those around her. We decided that she needed to set boundaries in her relationships, to be more careful about when and where it was appropriate to share her knowledge. We found that her current workplace was not the right forum to express her awareness. This also applied to some of her friendships outside of work.

Debbie is now on a path to utilize her gifts in a way that can be recognized and appreciated. She is considering going back to school to become a certified counselor, a profession that would allow her to work with others in a way that would be more fulfilling. I have found that High Priestesses are often service-oriented and working with others is deeply gratifying. Thus they tend to gravitate towards healing professions. Their ability to listen, to reflect to others their own journey of wisdom, is the mark of a High Priestess and of a healer.

Getting in touch with your High Priestess energy requires solitude. This card can represent the need for a time-out from relationships, work, and the outside world in general. This is a time to create an internal sacred space where you can commune with your deeper self. True spiritual empowerment—the very essence of The High Priestess—is the ability to be centered and connected to one's inner sense of knowingness.

Carl Jung, the famous Swiss psychoanalyst, could be seen as a modern day High Priestess in male form. Jung was interested in the occult, astrology, and alchemy. His work has greatly influenced our modern-day interpretations of the Tarot. When reading his sublime autobiography, *Memories, Dreams and Reflections,* I felt validated as a High Priestess, perhaps for the first time. Here, Jung speaks in personal terms of the timelessness of symbols and imagery, what he describes as archetypes, and how they spark recognition within our psyche. Jung stresses the importance of inward vision, saying, "My life has been singularly poor in outward happenings. I cannot tell much about them, for it would strike me as hollow or insubstantial! I can only understand myself in the life of inner happenings." It was Jung that first coined the term Collective Unconscious, similar in concept to the Akashic Records.

In traditional astrology, each sign and planet of the Zodiac is assigned a specific gemstone, and this can be applied to the Tarot as well. Ruled by the moon, The High Priestess's gemstone is a pearl. I mention this fact of gemology because The High Priestess is so like a pearl. You could say it is her talisman. The High Priestess is like a piece of sand hidden away in a shell and waiting in the ocean to be discovered. It is only with time that she becomes a great beauty, appreciated, and priceless. The pearl waits for its moment. Sometimes we need to smooth out the rough edges, to grow into our time. I have found it is easier to fulfill one's High Priestess energy as we grow older and mature.

III—The Empress

I n comparing The Empress with The High Priestess (the Women of the Tarot), one finds The Empress is inherently multiple while The High Priestess is alone and singular. The Empress's path represents an opening of self to others. She symbolizes the ability to not only nurture and give love, but to *receive* it as well.

The Empress is a celebration of the feminine. Sometimes this can be best expressed through relationships with female friends. There are times when one just needs to worship the Goddess with others. And what better way than to hang out with the girls, get a pedicure or makeover, shop, drink some wine, and share the nitty-gritty about your lover, boyfriend, husband, or lack thereof. This is a Venusian pleasure, a rite of womanhood.

This card represents feminine power. The Empress embraces the timeless bounds of female relationships, the strength of female bonds that endure—women supporting and embracing each other through thick and thin and the difficult choices a woman must sometimes make to find and get what she truly needs in life and in love. Seasons change, men may come and go, and children grow older. I have personally found that opening oneself to the love and nurturing of female friends enhances relationships with our male counterparts. What is written here is the feminine perspective, but it can give men insights into relationships with the females in their lives.

The Empress is ruled by Venus, the planet in astrology representing love and desire. Today it can be related to our modern day mating rituals. That is, looking for a relationship. The energy of Venus is expressed through the four elements of Fire, Air, Earth, and Water. Which of the following elements best describes you and your attitude towards relationships? Fire is gutsy, creative, and fiercely independent—an act first, think later mentality. Earth is sensual, conservative, material, and strongly security-oriented. Air is intellectual, eccentric, idealistic, and sometimes has a fear of attachment. Water is traditional, deeply romantic, and even fanciful, seeking a dream of love.

To explore your feminine energy check out the sign and element of Venus in your astrological chart and compare it to the placement of your moon. (For more information on how to get your chart see the "Astrology Wheel Spread" on page 33.) The moon represents your inner relationship with the feminine, emotions and intuition, your deepest self. Venus represents the outer expression of the feminine principal; it could be described as you in relationship with others.

I have a client named Gwen whose journey is a beautiful portrayal of The Empress. Gwen is 50-something, although she looks a good deal younger. Like The Empress, she is luminous in her being and radiates a serene beauty. Gwen is an artist and the single mother of a special needs child whom she has struggled to raise and support alone. She has experienced scarcity and a lack of abundance in her life, yet she has remained gracious and loving to those around her. Grace under pressure would be an apt description.

Gwen is a giver by nature. She often takes the role of caretaker and loves to help people. She worked full-time as a nurse's assistant in a retirement community, but found time to volunteer at her son's school and be available to the other mothers for support. Between her work, her child, and helping others, she had little time for herself, let alone her artwork, which she said was the closest she got to nurturing herself. Practicing her art had become a luxury, yet it was essential to her well-being. Gwen had been in survival mode for so long, she had almost forgotten what it was like to be on the receiving end of love.

I have watched Gwen evolve over many years, gradually transforming into an Empress in full bloom. Happily, she is now coming into her own. Her son has come of age and is living on his own in a special group home. Gwen is finally beginning to receive recognition for her art, and her goal is to become a successful working artist. Recently, she and the man she has been involved with, who also has children, decided to marry and buy a house together. Her dream has always been to have a loving partnership in her life. She is learning to embrace personal success and abundance, a whole new process for Gwen.

The Empress can represent the different stages in a women's life: Virgin, Mother, and Crone. These different stages of the Empress resemble butterflies in their stages of metamorphosis, from gestation to full born flight.

What I have found in my work with clients who are mothers, especially older mothers, is that they can have trouble letting go of their children. I find it interesting that so often, much of the reading is spent dealing with the clients' kids, their relationships, their lives, their problems, rather than with the clients themselves. Love can be controlling. Though these Empresses want only the very best for their children, there is a time to trust and let go, to come back to one's own life, separate from the role of mother.

The other side of the same coin is the child needing to let go of the mother. The Empress card often denotes a strong or dominant mother influence. Just as the mother needs to set the child free, so must the child let go of his or her need for approval from the mother.

In the Universal Deck, The Empress is shown surrounded by the beauty of nature, reclining on a plush throne. She represents Mother Nature in her element. One example of this aspect of The Empress card is my good friend Sylvie, who recently purchased a home on an island off the coast of Washington State. I am a city girl, but after much pleading, she enticed me to take the ferry from Seattle to the island. This meant going outside of my comfort zone. Would there be a Starbucks out there in nature? I was concerned about the proper attire and what shoes to wear (her property is somewhat wild after all), but Sylvie said not to worry, that on the island, people aren't concerned with fashion or looks. She said, "Just come and enjoy yourself."

Sylvie recently quit her job as a corporate business manager. She had been on the professional fast track for years and she was tired and burned out. Sylvie's mother had recently passed on and left her a nest egg of money, allowing her to take some time off and explore her options. As a corporate type, Sylvie had worn business suits. Now when I met her, she was in jeans and a T-shirt. She had also changed her hair color, from a dyed blonde to her own natural grey, and was tentatively reveling in her natural state of beauty.

It was around the summer solstice that I first journeyed to the island. When I left the ferry and stepped onto Sylvie's property, I felt like I had sipped a magic potion—the magic of nature. I felt lighter and more relaxed, stripped free of my city pretensions, which suddenly seemed quite silly.

On Sylvie's property there was a garden of great beauty. This was no ordinary garden. It had been written up in magazines and won prizes. The garden came with the property; you could say that Sylvie inherited it. She said, somewhat whimsically, that the garden was filled with mischievous nature spirits and it seemed that they controlled what occurred in the garden. Sylvie had never gardened before she moved to the island but it quickly became her passion. At the same, time it was challenging. Deer and birds were eating her rosebushes. Flowers were wilting and needed constant attention. She had to contend with the laws of nature. In her professional life, Sylvie was often in an authority position, giving her a lot of control. Now she had to surrender and make a "pact" with the elements, which required her to work with the garden instead of trying to control it. Sylvie, who had always been somewhat of a diva, was engaged in a dramatic relationship with her garden.

Sylvie has always been extremely independent, capable, and self-sufficient. In the past, she had no need to receive help from anyone. She wanted to do everything herself, but was quickly learning that it wasn't possible. Now she is taking horticulture classes and has hired a professional gardener to help her. She also has a roofer, a plumber, and a real estate agent, and I believe she considers them all to be good friends and partners in her new life. She has learned to relinquish control and ask for help—to receive. In her process of tending home and garden, and ultimately herself, Sylvie became an Empress.

IV—The Emperor

W hereas The Empress represented the expression of one's feminine, The Emperor is the expression of our masculine energy. Here it may be helpful to define the difference between the two. Words traditionally associated with each are listed here.

Male	Female
Animus/Yang	Anima/Yin
Conscious	Unconscious
Active	Passive
Aggressive	Receptive
Self	Other
Light	Dark
Left Brain	Right Brain
Intellect	Intuition
Expression: Outer/Career	Inner/Personal
Planets: Mars/Sun	Venus/Moon
Elements: Fire/Air	Earth/Water

We all have a male and female component to our natures, psychologically and spiritually. The soul has no gender, yet there is usually a reason we choose one over another in life. This is to learn certain lessons through experience. Instinctively, and sometimes unconsciously, we tend to rely on, and be more comfortable with, one aspect of self than another. For example, some women exhibit traditionally masculine characteristics, such as being assertive, action-oriented, and take-charge types. Similarly, some men carry traditionally feminine traits, such as being sensitive, feeling-oriented, and nurturers. This is not to imply that these women are masculine in appearance, or that

THE EMPEROR.

these men are effeminate. In fact, the opposite is often the truth. What is described here is more an expression of one's deepest self or inner personality.

Pop-psychology books like the John Gray series *Men are from Mars, Women are from Venus*, although walking a fine line between practical knowledge and stereotype, explore some important truths, and to some of us, major realizations. I admit to having a copy of this book and to being intrigued enough to stay up late into the night reading it. These truths are that physically, by the nature of our sex, we are equipped with different capabilities, and by understanding our differences in nature, we are helped in our ability to relate to one another. On this path, the emphasis is on the masculine component and suggests that it is time to explore, and possibly redefine, our male energy.

Aries, the sign of the warrior, rules The Emperor. Aries loves to conquer new territory and explore new ground. Those with strong Aries (or male) tendencies can be growth oriented, which requires a need to focus on self. When channeled in a positive way this can be creative self-exploration and self-expression. When out of balance or negatively expressed, it can result in conflict with others, especially in regards to defining the need for individual space. Our world being in a state of war brings up The Emperor's shadow side, misuse of power, and aggression. Currently, we are experiencing the darker side of human nature.

Astrology is based on polarities, the symbiotic relationship between opposite signs of the Zodiac. Opposite signs share a common theme and bond around life issues, yet each approach it from opposite viewpoints. Opposite signs could be described as two sides of the same coin. The opposite sign for Aries is Libra, representing fairness and balance (see the Justice card). Libra rules the house of relationships and represents the symbolic dance of self (Aries) and other (Libra). This is knowing when to push forward and exert your power, and knowing when to take a step back and receive. Traditionally, Aries is a taker while Libra is a giver. Ultimately, the balance between both aspects is what we strive for. The Tarot's Emperor represents the possibility of a warrior at peace, drawing on Libra's capacity for tolerance and diplomacy toward others.

I have found that when the Emperor card comes up in a reading, it can represent those dealing with issues around their own personal authority, exerting their power to get what they need in life. Keith's story is one example of this. By profession, Keith is an acupuncturist, and at the time of his reading, was a new father. Becoming a father was something that he and his partner had waited a long time to make happen. They had delayed welcoming a child into thier lives until later in their lives, until they had achieved some measure of professional success and financial stability. They were ecstatic about the opportunity to parent and celebrated the birth of their daughter, but creating space in their lives for a child was a whole new experience, and there were some issues that needed to be resolved. They were used to being separate and independent beings, but now with a third party involved, they were forced to relate to each other in a new way.

After the birth of their daughter, they decided it was time for Keith's partner to go back to school and finish his degree. So it was up to Keith to be the sole financial support of the family. Like The Emperor, Keith is an astute businessman. Yet he was growing tired of always being the one to make things happen. The Emperor card can represent taking on too much responsibility to the determent of one's own needs. He wanted more time to explore his creative energy. He had developed an interest in sculpting and working with clay—an expression of his feminine. He found that there were simply not enough hours in the day to do everything. Conflicts with his partner, whether around child care, cleaning the house, or money management, were becoming commonplace.

Keith decided he needed to learn how to delegate, to share his responsibilities. He hired both a house cleaner and a finance manager. The result is that he and his partner are more at peace and have more time to spend with their beautiful daughter. He is now in the process of building a studio in his garage. Through reclaiming his power and authority regarding his needs, Keith is now a happy Emperor.

Another expression of The Emperor can be in conflicts with authority figures. An example of this is Sidney, a banker by profession. The banking arena, Sidney said, is an Alpha male environment often based on the "old boys' network." Sidney could be described as a people pleaser, representing the qualities of the diplomatic and friendly Libra. She avoided conflict, and was often fearful of upsetting others. The result was that she turned over her power in many business situations. Sidney is a petite woman and sometimes felt physically intimidated by the men around her.

Some background on Sidney's life is helpful in understanding this state of affairs. Her father was a powerful presence in her life while growing up. He was a career military man who was dictatorial and insisted that his children played by the rules. Breaking them led to punishment, so at an early age, she learned to it was best to keep quiet and not express her opinions. The corporate environment, though, required Sidney to have a take-charge attitude, especially in regard to getting new business, a key component to her career success. She was well-liked, but did not want to step on toes, usually taking a back seat to others.

In her reading, we discussed the possibility that, as an adult, she had chosen the male corporate environment as a way of learning about her male energy, and that it offered her the opportunity to heal. Sidney is now taking classes in self-defense and martial arts. As a result, she feels less physically intimidated and is also experiencing a greater sense of balance between her male and female energy. She is in the process of claiming authority regarding her life choices, which for much of her life have been dictated by others—originally her father, and ultimately other authority figures around her.

The Emperor card is often about authority issues. In Keith's case, it meant that he had taken on too much authority and needed to back off to find a better balance in his life. In Sidney's, it meant that she needed to take more power and authority in her life. In the best sense, The Emperor can be described as representing balanced authority.

V—The Hierophant

T he Hierophant is the Spiritual Father of the Tarot and can be compared with The High Priestess, who is the Spiritual Mother of the deck. The Hierophant, or Pope, is the *external* expression of one's spirituality, whereas The High Priestess, or Popess, symbolizes the *internal* expression of one's spiritual nature. Those who relate to this card are often considering expressing their spiritual attributes to the outside world. With this card there is often the desire to, in some way, influence and guide others in their journey through life, incorporating a spiritual perspective. The path of The Hierophant emphasizes spiritual growth through teaching and learning. In reaching out to others and expressing faith in their divine potential comes the opportunity to find the sacred within oneself. In the highest sense, this represents the true nature of spirituality and is the essence of a spiritual teacher.

When we think about a spiritual teacher, religious leaders may come to mind, as the Pope is one. But a spiritual teacher may come in many forms. Their influence is not confined to those in a position of worldly power and importance, but may be seen in many walks of life, from the high school basketball coach who takes extra time guiding a young player when he needs it the most, to the business executive who volunteers on the weekends teaching literacy to adults. Spiritual teachers are not confined to traditionally spiritual venues. Also, spirituality and religion can be quite different. Both involve an exploration of the sacred and one's connection to the Divine. Yet whereas spiritually is the expression of a personal belief in spirit and its influence in life, religion implies certain dogma, and to some, a limited structure, which must be transversed on the path to the Divine.

THE HIEROPHANT

An example of a non-secular spiritual teacher is Deepak Chopra, the prolific author of such popular books as *How to Know God: The Soul's Journey Into the Mystery of Mysteries*. His influential work combines the spiritual with the material, blending Eastern wisdom with Western science. His work focuses on the mind-body-spirit connection, the power of conscious spirituality and intention, especially in regards to how this affects our health and well-being. Chopra's influence is widespread, as demonstrated by the overwhelming success of his many books, wellness center, and the Global Network for Spiritual Success. The Hierophant relates to finding our spiritual community and family, which again may adopt different forms and venues. Chopra is not a religious leader, but through his "ministry," he has influenced many to find and apply the spiritual in everyday life.

One definition of The Hierophant is as a "bringer of light." Those who are spiritual teachers help to illuminate profound wisdom in others. In addition to The Hierophant, there are several other cards in the deck that could also be described as light bringers and spiritual teachers: The High Priestess, representing the psychic or intuitive component to understanding the Divine: The Hermit, the behind-the-scenes mentor who is often tested in his faith; and the paths of Luminaries, especially The Star with its emphasis on teaching through inspiration.

An example of the Hierophant as spiritual teacher in everyday life is Michaela, a practitioner in the Chinese art of Feng Shui. This is an ancient system (some would say sacred) based on the belief that alternating the flow of energy (or chi) in the environment can produce desired change. The end result is health, happiness, and prosperity in one's life. Michaela had studied this art as an apprentice with several teachers and mentors for many years. In her reading, The Hierophant indicated that now it was time for Michaela to become the teacher. We discussed that going into people's homes and working with them to understand how they interacted with their environment was a way of helping others on a profound level, that in a sense, she was a spiritual teacher. Michaela was surprised by this comment, saying, "But I'm not religious." This again brings up the confusion between spirituality and religion. Her work and her ability to illuminate wisdom and help others to improve their environments and thus themselves, was highly spiritual in nature.

The shadow side of The Hierophant can be seen in the guru phenomenon, cult leaders of spiritual and religious movements who require turning over one's personal power to follow their version of spiritual beliefs and teachings. This includes some who take spiritual teachings and twist them into paranoid interpretations about the supposed end of the world and the extreme measures their followers must take to "save themselves." This is a form of spiritual insanity. The Hierophant represents spiritual authority. This requires asserting our authority in how we choose to explore our spirituality, and not turning our power over in the process.

In a Belgian deck of Tarot cards from the 18th century, the fifth Arcanum, what is traditionally called The Hierophant or The Pope, is instead entitled "Bacchus." The image shows Bacchus in full drunken regalia, wearing a wreath of grape leaves, sitting on a cask of wine, and drinking decadently from a flask. Each deck of cards carries the imprint of its designer, and in the evolution of the Tarot, different cards have carried different titles, focusing on certain aspects of their symbolism. This interpretation is unique and presents an interesting correlation between spiritual exploration and decadence. Bacchus is the Roman equivalent of Dionysus, the God of the Vine. In her book *Mythology: Timeless Tales of Gods and Heroes,* Edith Hamilton describes the ancient worship of this deity, especially in regard to the heady Dionysian Festival, as having two very different outcomes—the freedom and ecstatic joy of releasing one's inhibitions and desires, and the savage brutality that this may entail.

This may bring to mind The Devil card and its ruler Capricorn—the randy goat and its association with the fertility god, Pan. The Hierophant is ruled by Taurus, the sign of the bull, and an Earth sign like Capricorn. Earth signs are corporal and sensual, and the exploration of the tactile senses is an important part of understanding their true nature. In ancient times, the bull was associated with moon goddesses and was an important symbol in their fertility rituals. Taurus is ruled by the planet Venus, reminding us of The Empress card where we learned that love and desire go hand in hand with the body and nature and that all are paths for Divine exploration.

The Catholic priesthood requires celibacy. This is not the forum for a political discussion, yet when the natural senses of the body are repressed or presented as evil, it can lead to profound confusion about our bodies and self-expression. The priesthood is a symbol of goodness and order, yet it carries a shadow of secrecy. The Tarot, like all ancient systems of spiritual knowledge, has been influenced by church doctrine. I have a few clients who are Catholic, and to some, having a Tarot card reading is perfectly okay, while others have trepidations about the process. Perhaps they were taught that divination is the devil's work. Order and chaos, light and dark, good and evil—in the duality and balance of life, one cannot have one element without the other, and this could be described as the different reflections of the Divine.

In many religions, to commit to becoming a priest requires not only taking vows of celibacy and obedience, but also of poverty. In the Hierophant, this can be translated to becoming an empty vessel—free of pretension and material greed—in order to receive the gifts of spirit. This requires letting go of control and having faith that, one way or another, our needs will always be provided for when we are in the presence of the Divine. Taurus is a money sign, meaning it often places great emphasis on material comfort. To experience spiritual abundance one does not have to forgo money and security. In fact, it can mean the very opposite. Spiritual abundance means being rich in spirit.

The following joke seems appropriate in illustrating the true spirit of the Hierophant. There was a young scribe in training to become a monk. He had labored for several years, copying ancient texts of spiritual scripture, all the while giving up many of the corporal experiences of life. This included being celibate, which he assumed was a part of his training. One day, the head monk came in and asked the young scribe if he had read the holy book that was hidden away in the vault. Intrigued, the scribe went into the vault and was gone for some time. Finally, when he emerged, there was a huge smile on his face. When the Monk asked why, the scribe said, "It says *celebrate* (not celibate)!"

VI—The Lovers

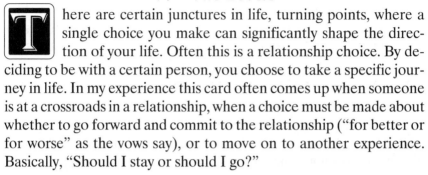here are certain junctures in life, turning points, where a single choice you make can significantly shape the direction of your life. Often this is a relationship choice. By deciding to be with a certain person, you choose to take a specific journey in life. In my experience this card often comes up when someone is at a crossroads in a relationship, when a choice must be made about whether to go forward and commit to the relationship ("for better or for worse" as the vows say), or to move on to another experience. Basically, "Should I stay or should I go?"

In the Marseilles Tarot, The Lovers card shows a man choosing between two women: a maiden and a crone. The women represent two different experiences or directions that the man can take. Symbolically, they represent the choice between innocence and reason. In this deck, a blindfolded Cupid is posed with his arrow of love waiting to strike. The Universal deck shows a winged angel. Both represent love just waiting to happen, a time to decide if you will be ruled by choice or give in to the winds of fate.

Sometimes the Lovers card represents a relationship triangle. For example, if you (or the person you are involved with) are dissatisfied, there may be a tendency to project unfulfilled desires or expectations onto someone outside of the relationship. Simply stated, you may be pulling in a third party to catalyze or define the relationship, one way or another.

The Lovers is about choice. So how does free will versus fate come into play? For example, from a historical perspective, if you were a peasant in 12th century France, there would not be much choice as to the outcome of your life. Because of the time you were born into, class distinctions, and political and economic restrictions, your destiny would be somewhat predetermined. There would be little free will involved. The age we live in is different, and the watchers and prophets of our time say there is currently a huge karmic release happening in our universe, that we must transcend karma (our prede-termined fates) in order to save the planet. No matter your spiritual or personal philosophy, this is obviously a time of great change on our planet, a time where humankind has choices to make about the outcome of our destiny. There are many choices, too many some would say, about our lives' directions and outcomes.

Sometimes in readings I hear the crossroads presented in The Lovers from clients who are in relationship dilemmas. "I just know that he (or she) is my soul mate, doesn't that mean something?" Yes it means something, but it is not an excuse to stay in a situation that is stagnant or counterproductive. It does raise the question, "Is there a person, one specific person, who is our destiny?"

The concept of soul mates and twin souls is intriguing, espe-cially to anyone seeking that one true love. There are many astrolo-gers, psychics, and spiritualists who put much stock into the concept of soul mates and twin souls, the idea that there is someone out there somewhere who is your other half, a person or soul who would somehow be a completion of yourself—your destiny.

The Garden of Eden symbolized a state of cosmic union be-tween Creator and humankind, a state of perfect being. It has been suggested that the separation of the sexes came from a desire for knowledge and experience of the opposite, symbolized by Eve eating the forbidden fruit from the Tree of Knowledge. This was the sup-posed beginning of opposites, of male and female. A twin soul could be described as your opposite self, your counterpart, a split that occurred in the pursuit of seeking knowledge of male and female energies. It is said that one is intrinsically drawn to one's "twin," and with this person, one may find a shared or common experience that is unexplainable in its synchronicity. The mirror that a twin soul can provide is a lesson that comes from the reflection of one's truest self. Yet these relationships can prove to be difficult on an intimate level and are not necessarily meant to last forever.

It is thought by some that when the Creator made the universe, it did so with duality in mind. The Earth plane was created in duality, the balance of opposites. A soul mate is the spilt that occurred in the original birth or incarnation. A soul mate is a separation of the soul, a necessary split for a deeper experience of the earth plane.

Once again, there is often a feeling of immense affinity with a soul mate, and they can represent opportunities, gifts, and milestones on the path of self-knowledge. Both soul mates and twin souls indicate a destined or karmic crossing of paths. Free will comes into play in your decisions about how you will choose to travel the lessons of these predestined "meetings." Either way, twin soul or soul mate, there is an essential split, a feeling of separateness that can result in a desire for completion of oneself through another.

The Tree of Knowledge of Good and Evil represents a desire for knowledge or experience. We are all looking for our "other half." We all have the need to experience wholeness with another. Yet, if we can find this completion within ourselves, we are free to love another without the baggage of unfulfilled expectations.

Princess Diana's story serves as a wonderful example of modern lovers and choices. The marriage of Lady Diana Spencer and Prince Charles tapped into a collective fantasy about love, romance, and happily ever after. It captured the imagination of a world that longed for a fairy tale, the very reason why so many romance novels are sold. Lady Diana was truly a princess looking for her knight in shinning armor to sweep her off her feet. Millions of people watched her storybook wedding on television. It was hard not to get caught up in the pageantry, watching the whole spectacle with a flutter of the heart, a collective sigh of, "What if that was me?"

At the time that Lady Di met Prince Charles, she embodied the hopes and dreams of many women. She was young and innocent, her head filled with fantasies of love and marriage. Yet the fairy tale quickly turned sour as reality and disillusionment set in. Prince Charles was not Prince Charming after all. Ultimately, these were two people very ill suited for one another, especially in regards to the realities of day-to-day life. Alas, the spell was broken, no happily ever after.

Unfortunately, because of Diana's death, we will never get to see what choices the Princess of Hearts, as she became known, would have made about her relationships in the future. When Diana died, perhaps so did a collective belief in fairy tales. On some level, we were all forced to redefine our perspectives on love and marriage.

In the world today, 40 percent of marriages are arranged. This practice is more prominent in Eastern cultures than in the West, perhaps making it difficult to grasp for those of us raised in Western homes. Arranged marriages are based on cultural and class similarities, criteria that may seem antiquated to some. I recently discussed the concept and practice of arranged marriages with a young man from India. He described to me, enthusiastically and in some detail, his search for the perfect wife. He had lived in the America for more than 10 years and although he liked free-spirited and independent American women, he said he wouldn't consider marrying one. He felt that American women were fickle, that they had too many choices and options, and this did not suit him. His family was in the process of casting horoscopes to find the right woman for him.

Today, the rules and expectations surrounding relationships and marriage are changing. The concept of spiritual partnership, a relationship based on independence and equality where both partners are empowered, is fast replacing traditional marriage.

Older generations, our parents for example, did not have the choices we do. An example lies in the story of how my parents came to be married. My mother and father are complete opposites. She is outgoing, at the time, an artist and a tomboy. He, no retired, was an engineer, conservative, and the strong, silent type. On their first date (a blind date), my father told my mother she talked too much. (She married him anyway.) When my father proposed to my mother, she literally had a plane ticket to Europe in her pocket. Her choice was to either marry my father or travel Europe. She chose my father. When asked why, to this day she says, "Chemistry." I do not believe that my mother is just referring to sexual chemistry, although I'm sure it had something to do with it, but a personal alchemy between the two of them. Perhaps, if my mother had not chosen my father, she would be an artist living in Europe or some other exotic location. My mother has often stated that she has never regretted her choice and that she would have it no other way. But it does make one think, "What if?" I have often heard it said that life is something that happens to us, separate from our best-laid plans. I think my parents would say they are happy with the outcomes of their lives. Are they one another's destiny? The answer to that question must be yes, for they chose to be.

Here we are, speaking of lovers, and love has been little mentioned. But then The Lovers is not about romantic love. The Lovers card is about a deep and influential learning experience, and what better way to experience it than through the amazing journey of loving another? Love is not perfect, it is not meant to be. Perfect or romantic love is an illusion. Ultimately, The Lovers is about trusting and finding peace with one's relationship choices.

Try using the Lovers Spread to explore your relationships more deeply. This will give you more information about your situation and also your probable future.

VII—The Chariot

he Chariot represents a subliminal journey of the unknown, offering the opportunity for self-discovery along the way. This card's association with Cancer relates to the realm of the unconscious and reminds us of certain aspects of The Moon card (in astrology, Cancer is ruled by the moon). The Moon's enigma is a mirror of the conscious and unconscious minds and shows the perils of the soul in negotiating the two. As the unconscious becomes defined, as it does on this path, we must sometimes face old dilemmas, ghosts from the past, especially in regards to family. Cancer has much to do with home and family, and here it may represent issues of separating from one's origins in the process of individuation. This can mean addressing unfinished business with one's family. The focus of The Chariot card is on new experiences, but it is important to not go forward with old baggage, as it will only weigh down our progress.

THE CHARIOT.

Sometimes one must go home again, at times literally, but here more in a psychological sense, to have the opportunity to rediscover oneself. This can present quite the conundrum of old and new, which may feel like finding a needle in a haystack. This is a process that will require the application of both inner and outer instincts, of mind and soul. As in The Moon card, defining boundaries is of utmost importance. Taking authority in matters and not seeking validation outside of oneself allows for a process of self-recognition where we become the masters of our destiny. This may require standing up for yourself in the face of adversity and being brave about what you believe to be true for yourself. In some sense, we are all seeking home. Here, it relates to the home within. By owning and defining oneself, we come closer to creating a foundation of authentic self—one's true home. This is a worthwhile endeavor that fulfills the promise of The Chariot's path.

The Charioteer's motto: "To thine own self be true," comes from William Shakespeare's *Hamlet*, a family tragedy of epic proportions. Shakespeare believed that world is a stage and we are players in the drama of life. On this path, we are the playwrights in a process of determining our destiny by the very choices we make in the moment. The stage may be set, but we as the authors of the play have much to say in character development and the direction of the plot. There is no established plan for this journey, yet here we are, encouraged to take charge of the course of defining fate. The Chariot mirrors Hamlet's most famous soliloquy as we ask the eternal question, "To be or not to be." *To be* can only come from a process of knowing, truly knowing, one's self. On this journey we must be prepared to face elements, both internal and external, that will challenge our character, but the end result can be the accomplishment of knowing that we have given the best effort on our own behalf.

In one's journey through the mysteries of the Tarot, it can sometimes be interesting to use other oracles, in conjunction with your process of discovery, to explore shared common themes and denominators. Just as we have linked Shakespeare's Hamlet with the Chariot card, here we can learn through different associations.

The Runes and the I Ching, like the Tarot, are ancient methods for seeking guidance in exploring one's destiny and they share similar spiritual truths. I have a number of clients who like to use these oracles with the Tarot to give them more perspective. Usually, this is in the process of divination and the only caution lies in going overboard and getting too much information. However, used properly and with some restraint, these oracles can combine to give you a different perspective on the situation you are exploring. The way to do this is to pick a Rune, or throw the coins for the I Ching, and see how they relate to your chosen card. You may be surprised at the results, especially at how these different systems can work together to give you insight. I have found that there is often an uncanny synchronicity between them. If this is not initially apparent, it may be revealed later as you go about the process of your life.

While working on The Chariot card, I decided to throw the coins and consult the I Ching as I sometimes do when seeking a different perspective. The I Ching, or Book of Change as it is called, uses hexagrams and a process of throwing coins to determine outcomes. It focuses on applying specific truths to help understand different situations. R. L. Wing's *I Ching Workbook* (Doubleday, 1979) is used here, but like the Tarot, there are many worthwhile books on the subject. The Hexagram that came up was #56 *TRAVELING*. This hexagram had interesting correlations to the essence of The Chariot card. This hexagram states:

> The time of *TRAVELING* is primarily a state of mind, yet it leads the traveler into very real spaces. Proper attitudes are of vast importance when moving through both time *and* space....

It finishes with:

> This could be a phase in your life when you are making an inner voyage, exploring new ideas, fantasizing new experiences, perhaps a new career or role. It may be that you see mundane day-to-day situations in a strange new light. If this is not a passing mood, it could mark the beginning of an identity crisis. Whatever is up, hold to your integrity—it may become your lighthouse in the seas of the unknown.

In this card, we become *travelers* exploring new life dimensions. This hexagram's reference to "proper attitude" and "integrity" is appropriate to The Chariot's path. Being truthful with and honoring oneself is the name of the game, the hallmark of this card. Redefining your new self through different and unknown experiences can sometimes result in an identity crisis. In The Chariot, we conquer our fears of the unknown. *TRAVELING* calls this the "seas of the unknown," which is another way of describing the watery Cancerian aspects of the card.

I have found that The Chariot often comes up in a reading when the seeker is facing issues around personal integrity. It often represents defining character moments in life that can effect one's reputation. Each card of the Tarot carries with it certain tests. Here, it is to be true to yourself.

An example of this aspect of The Chariot card is Kevin's story. Kevin is an entrepreneur in corporate training who started his business on a shoestring, and although he was experiencing some success with his work, found himself to be always just one step ahead of his creditors. At the time of his reading, he had been offered a new job working for a large company in a good position that offered a lot of money and prestige. He was torn. To take the job required a move—The Chariot may denote a move to a different location—and also giving up his own business to work for someone else. Kevin admitted that he was excited about the prospects that this new opportunity presented, but was worried about taking care of those he owed money. Could or should he abandon those who supported him in order to move on to greener pastures? This was obviously a complicated situation.

Kevin is a person who prides himself on his integrity. Ultimately, he decided to be true to himself and take the new job. But he used his advance from the company to pay off his old debts. This left him with no money to start his new life, but he felt satisfied that he had done the right thing, both for himself and others. Thus he could begin this new chapter with a clean slate, which was important to him. I considered Kevin's actions to be a most heroic effort.

The Chariot is symbolic of the hero journey. The conquering hero is an ancient archetype who shows up in myths, legends, and folk tales. The conquering aspect reminds us of this card's connection to The Emperor because on this path we need the instincts of a warrior to achieve our goals. In mythology, the hero journey involves many trials and tribulations where he faces great peril and adversity along the way. Here, the hero must overcome internal struggles with self in order to define his character. As the Emperor Napoleon Bonaparte once aptly stated, "Character is fate." By defining one's character, the hero may become worthy of the adulation of kings. This journey represents both the battle with material enemies outside of oneself, and also coming to terms with the inner and spiritual enemies within. The latter is the first objective that the hero must conquer, for without the foundation of personal integrity, the outside battle would be only one-dimensional.

VIII—Strength

he Strength card is ruled by Leo, the sign of the Zodiac symbolizing the heart. This card often indicates matters of the heart, though not necessarily of relationship love as one may initially think, but more of a love for self. Leos are often generous and bighearted people. They can be brave and strong creatures—the term "lion hearted" comes to mind. Yet underneath the surface, they also tend to be vulnerable and extremely sensitive. Leo is the sign of the Zodiac representing children, and indeed this sign often has a playful child-like nature that can be bruised easily. This card may indicate a wounding of one's heart, often occurring in childhood. When the early environment does not encourage individuality and creative expression, it can be deeply hurtful. Leo is ruled by the sun (see The Sun card) and these types need to express themselves, to be seen and acknowledged for their gifts. When this aspect of self is not nurtured or encouraged, it can be our first heartbreak, a deep wounding of the creative self. Sometimes this lack of attention can translate to a feeling of being inadequate, where individuals feel selfish or bad about their needs. This may translate to self-esteem issues. "I'm not good enough," or "My needs are not important."

Leos are sometimes seen as attention-getters because they often seek love and attention outside themselves. In reality, what they are looking for is recognition of self. The remedy is to find this love and acknowl-edgement within. Like the lion in The Strength card, Leos are fiery and passionate individuals who require a lot from themselves and others. This is both their karma and the essence of their strength.

The best way I can explain the wounded child aspect of this card is through the beloved tale *The Little Prince*, by Antoine de Saint-Exupéry. This is a story of a disillusioned man, an artist, who felt alone and misunderstood by other adults of the world. He found love and recognition for his "inner child" in his meetings with the strange and sweet little boy who came from a star in a galaxy far, far away. The vulnerability of the little prince, whose loyalty to a single flower left behind on his star, taught the man about the bittersweet nature of love and true compassion. Antoine de Saint-Exupery used the following dedication in his book:

> To Leon Wirth. I ask the indulgence of the children who may read this book for dedicating it to a grown-up. I have a serious reason: he is the best friend I have in the world. I have another reason: this grown-up understands everything, even books about children. I have a third reason: he lives in France where he is hungry and cold. He needs cheering up. If all these reason are not enough, I will dedicate the book to the child from whom this grown-up grew. All grown-ups were once children—although few of them remember it.

This story is a reminder of the importance of nurturing the child-like parts of self.

Mia came to me for a reading during a "healing crisis" in her life. I use this term because her situation was opening up old wounds that needed to be healed. She was in the process of breaking up with a long-time love and was dealing with issues surrounding her self worth. Her relationship had been painful for some time and wasn't meeting her needs, but she felt reluctant to leave, hoping that things would get better. This is a familiar scenario to those of us who have stayed too long in painful relationships. In her reading, we discussed that Mia's loyalties were unbalanced, having excluded her own needs, and also remembering that she deserved love that made her happy. She knew this intellectually, but dealing with her emotions was another matter.

Born in Greece, she came to this country as a child. She is a handsome, strong-featured woman, whom I would describe as exotic looking, but she said she has always felt ugly, especially in comparison with the "Anglo" women she grew up with. She was orphaned by the deaths of her parents while a teenager and talked about how alone and empty she felt. She was struggling with an eating disorder, replacing love with food, trying to fill a void deep inside, and she felt terrible shame and guilt about her secret addiction. The Strength card indicated that to heal her wounds she needed to learn how to love herself. This process made her feel deeply vulnerable, requiring her to draw on her inner strength.

In my office, I have a picture of Quan Yin, the Chinese Goddess of Compassion, and Mia was quite taken with it. One day I was shopping at my favorite bookstore and found a small statue of Quan-Yin carved in cherry wood. The figure showed Quan Yin pouring her healing waters over a fierce but subdued dragon. It reminded me of the image of The Strength card and also of Mia. On a whim, I decided to buy it for her. When I gave it to her, she broke into tears. This small gift meant so much to her. Mia decided to create a heart altar and used the statue of Quan Yin as the central piece, including other personal items that represented love and nurturing, giving her comfort in her journey of learning self-compassion.

Some time later, I received a long letter from her postmarked from Greece. In the letter, Mia explained that one day while meditating at her altar she had a vision of herself as an adult sitting on a rocky sunlit beach in her homeland. This vision inspired her to travel to Greece and connect with long-lost relatives. Finding her extended family made her feel like she had finally found her authentic self. Mia's story fits nicely with another treasured children's tale, Hans Christian Andersen's *The Ugly Duckling*. We all know the story of the duckling who was seen as awkward and was shunned by the other ducks in the pond. Then, much like Mia, through time and patience, he was transformed into a beautiful swan. In the process of acting on her desire for a new life, one more in accordance with her true needs, Mia felt loved and accepted for the first time in her life. She became a swan.

When this card comes up in a reading, it represents a time for a loving and thoughtful focus on self, to enhance the opportunity for creative self-growth. This often means putting yourself first. On this matter, what I sometimes hear from clients is that they are afraid of being seen as vain or overly selfish and they have guilt about spending time on their own needs. Here it is important to differentiate between selfish and self-full. The first may represent ego-greed, the desire for self-gratification. The latter represents paying attention to and honoring your needs, an essential component to a healthy sense of self-esteem. This requires trusting your instincts—your heart sometimes over your head—about what is right for you.

This card represents a process of getting in touch with our passion and desire. To know your passion, your heart, you have to know yourself. This is a journey of self-discovery, which was emphasized in the previous Arcanum, The Chariot. The Strength card, also know as Force, represents a time in our lives to not force anything: our process, our healing, or our growth. Like the maiden pictured in this card, we must be patient and compassionate with ourselves. Here, strength transforms into compassion, the willingness to love and nurture ourselves on the path to self-actualization. In Strength, we learn unconditional love for ourselves that then gives us a foundation in which we may find this with others.

IX—The Hermit

he Hermit is like The Fool in the sense that each hears a different drummer and follows their own beat or rhythm in life. These paths tend to be somewhat unique and individualistic in nature. Both are loners and separate from the fold. Both represent journeys into the unknown where faith is a key element. But whereas the Fool defiantly stands out in the crowd because he is different, the Hermit does not draw attention to himself. Instead, he wishes to vanish into the shadow. The shadow is The Hermit's home. To reveal himself can be almost painful, and it defeats his purpose. His very "invisibility" gives him the stealth to move in many circles, to observe and gather information without being seen. This is a valuable tool for self-realization.

Those with a strong connection to this card tend to be loners. Loners are not always alone, a common misconception. They can have great relationships and be an active part of the community, yet essentially they feel separate from others. In the best sense, The Her-

THE HERMIT.

mit values his relationship with self and enjoys being alone. This card reminds us to seek solitude, essential to the Hermit's nature. An extreme aspect of this card can be where one becomes too isolated. Hermits' primary relationships are with their higher calling. They can become so self-reliant and involved with their inner process that they become too separate.

In readings, The Hermit represents a time to seek inner solace, usually meaning needing more personal time for one's relationship with self. Or it can represent someone who is in a relationship, but feels separate from his or her partner—essentially alone. For some, The Hermit may represent the fear of never having a deep and meaningful relationship. In this process, there is often a need to let go of a belief of what a "perfect" relationship may be. It requires the willingness to explore unknown possibilities.

With this card I often hear, "What is my higher purpose in life?" I believe The Hermit comes up in a reading when someone is searching to understand his or her spiritual path. The Hermit's ruler, Virgo, governs the sixth house of the Zodiac representing "Health, Work, and Service." Virgos and Hermits tend to be service orientated. The idea of the sixth house is that doing fulfilling work leads to a sense of well-being, and thus good health. In regard to careers, Hermits are often well-suited to the roles of teachers and mentors. In the healing arts, they may be found as physicians, naturopaths, or nutritionists. Whatever their professions, Hermits often tend to be the people that we seek out for wisdom and advice.

An example of The Hermit is Sybil, a minister who works with the terminally ill in a hospice center. She came for a reading because she wanted to explore a change in career directions. Sybil loved her work, ministering to others, but she was burnt out from the extreme environment of her job. She was tired of being on the front lines and sought work that was less stressful, yet no less fulfilling. She had delayed coming for a reading because of her religious beliefs. As a practicing Catholic, there was no basis for this process, yet she was drawn to the mystical arts.

The experience of having a Tarot card reading was obviously a big deal and outside of her current realm of parameters. Sybil's question in the reading was, "What am I supposed to be doing with the rest of my life?" I asked her to shuffle the cards and focus on her question. Using the Destiny Spread (see page 30) worked well to explore Sybil's situation. The card that came up in the Soul (Past) position was The Death card. Sybil told me her beloved cat had recently passed on and she was beside herself with grief. She said that her cat's death was a sign to her that her life needed to change. The cat, her constant companion, had given her so much love that she now needed to find a way to be more loving towards herself. The Death card also represented her ability to work with others in an extreme time in their lives. But because Death was in a past position, it indicated it might be time to leave that work.

The card coming up in the Spirit (Present) position was The Hermit. For Sybil to quit her job and go in a new direction would require a great deal of faith, something she was keenly aware of. She was fearful of letting go of her present position, especially in regard to her monetary security. Even though she and her husband were well off financially, there was concern that this would put them into survival mode. This came from old conditioning. Her family had never had enough money, and her childhood had been based on scarcity. Sybil also admitted that her identity was very much associated with her current career, and to let it go made her feel anxious, especially because she didn't know what was next. The Hermit represented a time to embrace the unknown, to take a break from ministering to others, and spend more time with her own needs.

The card that came up in the Destiny (Future) position was the Strength card. When I asked her what she felt passionate about, Sybil said she was drawn towards a form of art therapy she was currently taking classes on. Hermits love to learn. This was a new model for therapy that used creativity to explore one's inner self. It had an esoteric bent that initially she wasn't sure about. In the process of learning it, Sybil realized that she had not thought of herself as a creative person. She recognized this as a wound and realized she had to believe in herself. She wanted to teach others this form of therapy. She loved the process of learning something new, but the idea that she would be able to teach it to others was daunting to her.

When I last saw Sybil, she had given notice at her job and was taking time to do her own artwork. She had also dedicated herself to learning more about art therapy. Even though she did not feel quite ready to make it her career choice, she felt that time would tell and was more at peace with her process.

As Hermits seek wisdom, there can be an over-emphasis on intellectual knowledge. This is represented by Virgo's tendency to over analyze and put emphasis on facts instead of experience. Beth's story is one example of this aspect of The Hermit. Beth was a student earning her master's degree in European history. Coming from a family of academics (both her mother and father are teachers), it was only natural that she follow in their footsteps and become a teacher herself. At the time of her reading, Beth wanted nothing more than to take a break from her studies but she was scared to disappoint her parents.

She wanted to travel Europe and experience first hand what she had studied. She wasn't sure what she wanted to be when she "grew up," but she wanted the time and space to define it, without the agendas of others.

In Beth's reading, The Hermit was joined by The Emperor card, representing a time where she needed to take power regarding her choices in her path and in life. Beth sometimes turned her power over to authority figures, not just her parents, but her teachers as well. She needed to become her own authority and define what was best for her, to trust herself and her own judgment. Beth decided to take a sabbatical from her studies and is planning a trip to Italy. She isn't sure where her path will take her, but she is excited about the prospect of discovery.

I have always been fascinated by the Arthurian Legends, especially the character of Merlin the Magician and how his essence embodies the archetype of The Hermit. Merlin has inspired the minds and imaginations of historians and mystics alike. There are many books dedicated to an exploration of Merlin's legend, and even a deck of Tarot cards in his name (The Merlin Tarot). As a young adult I read Mary Stewart's series on the Arthurain saga. Her first book, *The Crystal Cave*, is about Merlin's troubled boyhood as a bastard prince. Abandoned by his father (the prince of darkness) and left to his own devices, Merlin felt alone and separate from the rest of the world—misunderstood. In Mary Stewart's version of Merlin's story, he meets a wise hermit who lives in a cave. The hermit, Galapas, becomes his teacher, and with much patience and foresight teaches him the mystical arts. In Galapas's cave are crystals that lead to knowledge and illumination. Here, for the first time, Merlin feels at home. Merlin had "the sight," the ability to see what others could not, which had been disorienting to him, but he learned with his teacher's help how to use his gift.

Magic, wisdom, nature, and paying attention to the sound of every leaf and rock became synonymous with Merlin. We all know the end of the story where Merlin became the advisor, teacher, and mentor to King Arthur. Legend says that Merlin did not so much die, but was put to sleep. With his death it is said that so died the old ways of magic for the Druid sect and the pagan belief in magic and nature. Today, Merlin is often portrayed as the old wizard with a long beard wearing at tall pointy hat illustrated with stars. Although commercialized, the essence of Merlin the Hermit lives on. Mary Stewart says that someday Merlin will awaken again and "come back in the hour of his country's need."

X—The Wheel of Fortune

 e have all heard the phrases: "What goes around comes around," "We reap what we sow," and, "What goes up must come down." What you may not know is that they are all based on the universal Law of Karma. The Wheel of Fortune, or Karma as it is sometimes called, represents Divine Law, especially the Law of Karma. Karma is based on the cosmic and scientific principal of cause and effect: Every action generates a force of energy the must be completed in its counterpart. Many eastern religions use this law as the foundation of their spiritual belief system. The ancients saw the wheel as a symbol of the soul evolving through eternity from one lifetime to the next. But you don't have to believe in reincarnation to apply karma. By understanding this ancient law, we can make choices that help create successful lives.

Paramahansa Yogananda, in his book *Autobiography of a Yogi,* says: "Dharma (cosmic law) aims at the happiness of all creatures." Dharma relates to one's purpose and duty in life and to the idea that everyone has a unique talent and gift that, when fulfilled in service, leads to happiness and eternal well-being. All divine laws are applicable to this card. The following is an excerpt from Deepak Chopra's *The Seven Spiritual Laws of Success* as presented on his Website. His insights into the Law of Karma are a helpful tool to those embarking on the path of The Wheel of Fortune.

WHEEL of FORTUNE.

Applying the Law of Karma or Cause and Effect:
Witness Choices

1. Today I will witness the choices I make in each moment. And in the mere witnessing of these choices, I will bring them into my conscious awareness. I will know that the best way to prepare for any moment in the future is to be fully conscious in the present.

Evaluate Consequences

2. Whenever I make a choice, I will ask myself two questions: "What are the consequences of this choice that I'm making?" and "Will this choice bring fulfillment and happiness to me and also to those who are affected by this choice?"

Listen with Your Heart

3. I will then ask my heart for guidance and be guided by its message of comfort or discomfort. If the choice feels comfortable, I will plunge ahead with abandon. If the choice feels uncomfortable, I will pause and see the consequences of my action with my inner vision. This guidance will enable me to make spontaneously correct choices for myself and those around me.

The Wheel of Fortune is an active exploration of the concept of fate versus choice. We first experienced this theme in Arcanum six, The Lovers, where we realized that the choices we make in relationcan ships define our journey in life. Fate could be described as a predetermined order or outcome that is prescribed by a power outside, or greater than, ourselves. Choice involves freewill. Some aspects of life are predefined, but many are determined by the choices we make in each moment. This is free will. The ability to actively make choices with good intent for self and others can change both one's karma and one's destiny. Ultimately, as we will find in the next card, Justice, it is a balance between two truths: conscious choice, as the realization of our actions and their consequences, and the influence of predetermined outcomes or fate, as the belief in a bigger picture at work. It is this duality between opposite yet equal forces that makes the wheel spin and is aptly described in an ancient Muslim proverb that says, "Trust Allah, but always tie up your camel."

The Wheel of Fortune often represents the beginning of new enterprises in one's life. An example of this element of the card is Renee's story. Renee is a life coach who, through her one-on-one work with clients, writings, and workshops, has become a significant presence on the "new age" circuit. Before starting any new project,

Renee told me that she always says a prayer to Ganesh, the Hindu god of wisdom and knowledge. She even uses the image of this god on her business cards. Ganesh is the god with the body of a man and head of an elephant that is often portrayed riding on the back of mouse. Throughout the ages, this ancient god has garnered much affection as symbol of good luck and as a benevolent presence to evoke when embarking on new endeavors. Ganesh is still very popular today, with devotees creating everything from Websites to wallpaper in his image.

I do not consider Renee to be a superstitious person, or someone who would even believe in the fates. In the fact, just the opposite. As a smart, successful business person and a personal empowerment coach, she is someone who is all about creating opportunities and encouraging her clients to take the bull by the horns and make things happen in their lives. Yet her belief in a force greater than herself and her willingness to bring it into her life, to me, made her seem humble and more human, which nicely balanced out her powerful presence. Renee is indicative of the best use of The Wheel of Fortune— that Fortune is both created and divinely guided.

The Wheel of Fortune brings to mind images of gamblers playing at games of chance. Originally, Lady Luck, as she has come to be known, was Fortuna, the patroness of gamblers, and her fate wheel became the roulette wheel we see in casinos today. As billionaire businessman and casino owner Donald Trump would surely attest, there is a lot of money to be made from those who play with Lady Luck. Trump is a Wheel of Fortune in action, always playing the odds in his many business enterprises. Trump is a gambler at heart and seems to relish the power of the game. In his many experiences, with the ups and downs of fortune he always seems to be having fun, and his huge success comes from making the most of all opportunities. As my mother used to say, "He could make a silk purse out of a sow's ear," meaning that Trump can take even a worst-case scenario and make it work to his advantage. This path says to expect unexpected opportunities and fortunes. The outcome is determined by what you do with them. Sometimes you win, sometimes you lose, but like Donald Trump, you won't know the possibilities unless you are willing to play the game.

Country western singer Kenny Rogers immortalized the Gambler in his song of the same name with the line, "Know when to hold 'em, know when to fold 'em, know when to walk away and know when to run." This may sound silly, but there is a deeper truth here. The Wheel of Fortune is a path of risk, of laying your cards on the table and seeing what happens. This involves taking a risk in the probability that the outcome will be fortunate. On this path, flexibility is key and sometimes, like Rogers' "Gambler," you have to be willing to know when it's best to move on, to realize that there are just some things outside of your control. The Wheel of Fortune represents both a completion and a new beginning. Taking advantage of the opportunities on this path represents knowing when to end the game and begin a new one. By doing so, it offers the opportunity to release old, stagnant patterns in life and embark on new and possibly winning ones.

Doing a Tarot card reading is a Wheel of Fortune experience. Divination and fortune telling comes from the idea of exploring what fate may have in store for us. Sometimes in readings with clients, I notice a moment of hesitation after they have shuffled and cut the cards and are about to pick a pile. How do you know you will pick the right pile? Also they may wonder whether they have shuffled enough or correctly. It is always interesting to see the look of amazement on their faces when the cards appear in the right places of the spread addressing the very situation in their lives they wish to address. Is this coincidence or some form of magic? Not to burst any bubbles, but it is actually more scientific than that. Within the subconscious mind is the ability to arrange the cards exactly according to the right configuration needed in the moment. This concept is seen in the rare and genius ability of "card counters" in Las Vegas, who have the ability to mentally track the cards of a deck that have been played in a game. This gives them an advantage that makes them unwelcome in casinos. In all readings, I tell clients that the cards that come up in their reading are not accidents, and they must trust the higher mind's ability to present to us what we need to know. In a Tarot card reading, much like The Wheel of Fortune, one must take the hand that one is dealt and, most importantly, work with it and make it one's own.

XI—Justice

T hroughout the ages, we have been fascinated with justice and its proceedings. Everyone enjoys a good trial because we like to see justice served, and yet there can sometimes be a vengeful aspect to this process. Vengeance, the desire to right wrongs at all costs, is the dark side of justice. In ancient times, the Roman gladiators fought lions in a common court of judgment— the arena. A final thumbs up or thumbs down given by the Caesar (the judge of the proceedings), and the crowd, (the jury), decided the fate of the participant. In the movie *Gladiator*, Russell Crowe's character fought against the Empire in a savage portrayal of injustice. In the end, he avenged the wrongs done to himself and his family by taking justice into his own hands, all in the name of truth and honor. In real life, and in the path of Justice, we are encouraged toward a more balanced approach to seeking justice in our lives.

The previous Arcanum, The Wheel of Fortune, explored karma and the workings of Divine Law. The Justice card represents the desire for truth and fairness in our lives. In this process, sometimes we need to let go and adhere to the belief that what goes around will come around and ultimately a natural state of balance will be achieved. This requires belief in a higher order of justice and in an essential fairness in the universe. Only rarely, as in Crowe's gladiator, does taking extreme measures fulfill the need for true justice.

In the modern world, we have had many "trials of the century," from the Lindberg baby kidnapping to the O.J. Simpson murder trial. Simpson's "dream team" helped to make lawyers into celebrities, leading to the advent of a cable television network dedicated to trials: Court TV, where authorities pontificate on law and justice. In a sense, the climate for justice is now no less bloodthirsty, though more veiled in polite rhetoric, than in Roman times.

Many tire of the media's attention, some would say exploitation, of trials, celebrity and otherwise. With the relatively new phenomenon of "reality television" we have many shows focusing on different, and somewhat interesting, aspects of justice: the ever-popular Judge Judy, a tough, no-nonsense lady justice; *Divorce Court*, where people air their dirty laundry in the hopes of attaining justice; or even *Fashion Court*, where participants are judged on their fashion choices by both a judge and jury. Whatever the form, with these shows, we get to play armchair quarterbacks and judges in deciding the fate of the participant, reflecting an enduring if chameleon desire to see justice done.

Libra, the sign of the Zodiac associated with the planet Venus, rules the Justice Card. Venus represents the feminine, and the illustration of its connection to this card is stated best by the poet Keats who said: "beauty is truth and truth is beauty." The spirit and representation of Justice is usually as a woman: Lady Justice. Sandra Day O'Connor, as the first woman to be appointed to the Supreme Court, is a modern day Lady Justice. Lady Justice is pictured on this card holding a sword and a scale. Her sword has a double edge, representing both severity and mercy. The scales represent the balance between these two extremes. Rolla Nordic, in her book *The Tarot Shows the Path*, emphasizes the importance of both the mind and the heart in justice, saying, "The heart is very important in the achievement of balance and harmony. It must not rule the head. Every thought is recorded in the heart."

Justice begins the second half of the Tarot's Major Arcana and is the point of balance between the two. Paths zero (The Fool) through 10 (The Wheel of Fortune) represent the personal expression of the Tarot's mysteries. Paths 11 (Justice) through 21 (The World) are more universal in nature. In Justice, we begin to incorporate these two halves: the universal and the personal. This card represents a time to reevaluate and rebalance accordingly. In physical astrology, Libra rules the kidneys, the organ that functions in purifying wastes and toxins and eliminating them from the body. The Justice card represents a purge of sorts: One can expel the elements in one's life that are not working to find a new sense of centeredness.

The Justice card represents the need for balance, which may show up in our lives in different ways. Kathryn's story is one example of this. She is a client who was at a point in her life where she had to make some major decisions about her future, and she was vacillating between different courses of action. The Libra's doubled-edged sword is the ability to see both sides of a situation. Its gift is fairness, but at the same time, it can get caught up in weighing and balancing facts, leading to its curse—indecision. The card representing her in the reading was the Justice card, and this was appropriate, as Kathryn felt her process was out of balance.

Kathryn is a woman in her mid-30s, and she was experiencing chronic hip pain, which, according to her doctors, was unusual for someone her age. The cause of her pain, at times debilitating, was a mystery. In her session, we consulted Louise Hay's pioneering book on the body-mind connection, *You Can Heal Your Life.* Hay says that, ultimately, the hips "carry the body in perfect balance" and represent a "major thrust in moving forward." Hip problems, according to Hay, are based in "fear of going forward in major decisions." This fit Kathryn's situation perfectly. The affirmation for this conflict is, "I am in perfect balance. I move forward in life with ease and with joy at every age."

Kathryn realized, with a reminder from both the Justice card and Louise Hay, that she was going from one extreme to another in her decision-making process. This was not a judicial use of her energy and was throwing both her body and her being out of balance. She is now learning to take the middle road, trusting and being more at ease with herself as she contemplates her move into the future.

Lady Justice is also associated with Athena, the Greek Goddess of Wisdom. Athena is often shown with an owl on her shoulder. The owl has night vision and can see in the dark. It serves to light up Athena's blind side so she can see the whole truth, as opposed to only a half-truth. Justice is often seen blindfolded, representing her blindness to favors in her search for the truth.

As we have seen, this card rules courts and law and can sometimes represent legal proceedings. Another client, Laurie, was going through a bitter divorce when she came to me. Her situation was complicated because her husband, the chief breadwinner in the relationship, was being unethical regarding money. He had hidden away money that was unaccounted for, which would leave Laurie with little as they divided their assets. She was trying not to feel bitter, but she felt like her soon to be ex-husband, a powerful corporate attorney, was manipulating circumstances and exploiting the law in his favor. She was intimidated by her husband's power and his knowledge of the law. This represents another aspect of the dark side of justice, using the law for one's own purposes.

Laurie had admittedly been in denial for some time concerning her marriage and had blinded herself to the reality of the situation. She felt a conflict between her mind and her heart. One told her to leave, the other to stick it out. Libra is the sign of harmony and Laurie had been trying to keep things going in her marriage by not speaking up. In her reading, we discussed that, like the goddess Athena, she needed to both find and then speak her truth. In the process, Laurie was required to confront and defend her beliefs, becoming somewhat of an expert in divorce law.

Laurie represents an extreme example of the need to find the truth in life. When I last saw her, divorce proceedings were still in play, but she seemed more at peace knowing that, whatever the outcome, she had done the best she could. In a perfect world, her circumstances may have been different, but ultimately, she was willing to believe that what goes around comes around and that justice would be served.

XII—The Hanged Man

Each of the 22 cards of the Major Arcana are considered to be spiritual in nature, yet The Hanged Man is one of the most spiritual paths because it requires the surrender of one's will to a higher order or spirit. This process can be both liberating and challenging. The liberation comes from the unencumbered serenity of being at one with the Divine. The challenge lies in having to relinquish control in order to achieve this state. The dark side of The Hanged Man is martyrdom. Martyrdom implies sacrifice, often suffering, for a cause—sometimes religious, sometimes otherwise. Martyrdom is a tradition that has been with us since the beginning of human civilization. In present times, it can be seen in political prisoners who go on hunger strikes or the suicide bombers in the Middle East. These are extreme cases, but we can all be martyrs in our everyday lives as well.

Often when this card appears in a reading, the seeker is facing obstacles that may seem, at the moment, to be insurmountable. This can lead to a feeling of victimization, of being betrayed or deceived by life and being powerless to change the circumstances encountered. The key dangers on this path are despair, discouragement, and in some cases, beating up on oneself for things outside of one's control. This is where a spiritual perspective helps, the application of the belief in something greater than our present circumstances and ourselves. An important reminder on The Hanged Man's path is that we cannot always control what happens in life, but we can control how we react to the circumstances.

THE HANGED MAN.

We all have Hanged Man moments from time to time. What I have found to be most helpful on this path is to take a step back and truly surrender to a different perspective or approach to the difficulties of the situation. The remedy may be as simple as a good night's sleep, where we can detach and work through issues with the help of the subconscious mind. The result can be a renewed sense of well-being in the morning. Often what we really need is just a little tea and sympathy, so to speak. The offering of a kind word or a simple act of encouragement can make all the difference between despair and hope, someone saying: "It's okay, you're fine, and you're doing a good job." This may come in different ways from different sources. The key here is being open to hearing and receiving it, to letting help in rather than suffering alone.

Neptune rules The Hanged Man. In astrology, this planet represents spirituality, transcendental experiences, the unconscious, the psychic realm, unconditional love, creativity, fantasy, imagination, drugs, alcohol, and addictions. What all these elements share in common is the potential to transcend mundane reality and connect to something different or greater than ourselves. Obviously, some aspects are healthier than others. In esoteric astrology, Neptune is synonymous with soul. Some of our greatest mystics, artists, poets, and writers have a strong Neptune component to their astrology. What I have found to be helpful for those with a strong Neptune or Hanged Man aspect to their natures is to employ and explore creativity. Creativity gives us a way to connect to a higher plane in a healthy way.

The Moon card is also associated with Neptune, as is the Hanged Man through Pisces. There are some similarities between the two cards. Both represent an exploration of non-physical realms, which may involve dealing with illusions, whether real or of our own making. The counter effect of illusion is disillusionment, which can lead to the despair that is inherent to both paths. Here, talking with someone to gain a different perspective can be helpful. Or again, some form of creative expression can help us to explore our difficulties in a way that engages the imagination and encourages us to explore other possibilities.

Like Neptune, The Hanged Man can represent an element of escapism. In a healthy sense, this can be a desire to explore possible realities outside of our everyday mundane existence. The unhealthy expression comes in the form of wanting to check out from reality. Movie star Judy Garland's famous portrayal of Dorothy in *The Wizard of Oz* is an example of this. Her heartbreaking rendition of "Somewhere Over the Rainbow" reveals the urge to escape to a more perfect child-like world where life is simpler and "troubles melt like lemon drops." The colorful Land of Oz was quite different from Dorothy's harsh reality on Auntie Em's farm and the bleak, grey landscape of Kansas. The Hanged Man can represent the inclination to seek a more perfect world or different state of existence, sometimes with unrealistic expectations. What Dorothy found was that life in Oz was not so simple after all. On her journey, she had to face elements of herself that lead her back to the safe haven of her ordinary world. We may all wish to escape to other places from time to time, but what we often find is that ultimately, like Dorothy, we still have to face ourselves.

Judy Garland grew disillusioned with her journey in another Oz-like world—Hollywood. As a child actor, she had to meet Hollywood standards, subjecting her to its star-making machine and leading to crippling insecurities that highlighted deeper issues around her self-worth. We can all relate to the feeling of not being good enough and never living up to others' expectations. A healthy sense of self-esteem is essential to negotiating The Hanged Man's path, for without this, we can fall victim to the internalization of the needs of others. Garland was plagued throughout her life with many addictions, leaving her exhausted. Although she was always a trouper, in the sense that she never gave up but made the best of her circumstances, she died worn out from her journey in life. Garland's story represents a cautionary tale of The Hanged Man.

The Hanged Man card is extremely spiritual, which, when out of balance, can translate to spiritual extremes. For example, in olden times, there was a sect of monks that self flagellated to atone for their perceived sins. This is a form of self-crucifixion and martyrdom. The Hanged Man may represent feeling guilty for no good reason. On this path, guilt may be a signal and a red flag that it is time to take a step back and realign with your sense of worth. This is especially true in regard to taking care of the needs of others.

Teresa's story serves as an example of this. Teresa is a sweet woman who could be described as wearing her heart on her sleeve. She is always helping others and is the one who gives the money to the homeless person on the street. Teresa was not connected to any religion, but considered herself to be a spiritual person. Since childhood, she has had an affinity for the saintly Mother Teresa, her namesake.

At the time of her reading, she was experiencing difficulty in her personal and professional lives. Teresa is a massage practitioner and her finances were suffering because she often took clients who were late in paying, sometimes even giving away her services for free if someone couldn't afford them. In her personal life, she was in a relationship with a man who, although caring, was often so busy with his work that he did not have enough time for her. This left her feeling needy and out of control. Teresa had prayed to no avail for some sign of change. She said she felt forsaken by others and the world at large and admitted to feeling sorry for herself. She asked, "Why is this happening to me?"

In her session, we discussed that she needed to be more assertive about creating opportunities for herself. Teresa always believed that somehow, someway, Spirit would take care of her. The result was that she had turned over life to unseen and unknown forces that could not provide for her tangible needs. I also asked her to consider the possibility that she was making too many sacrifices for others, and that she might be asking too much of herself in this regard. Teresa said that she often felt guilty when not helping others and I pointed out that, although her intent to be of service was worthwhile, this could be a way of avoiding herself and not focusing on learning how to take care of her own needs. I brought up the idea that God helps those who help themselves, and this was a concept that spoke to Teresa. In the end, she realized that she needed to put herself first, in a sense to save herself.

In the best sense, The Hanged Man reflects the balance of the previous Arcanum, Justice, representing a balance between human and spiritual needs. A balanced Hanged Man represents healthy spiritualism. This can be seen in spiritual leaders who accept their human vulnerabilities as a part of their connection to the Divine. They do not suffer as much as inspire. The Hanged Man's number is 12. In numerology, this breaks down to three ($1+2=3$), which is the number for The Empress's path of love, a reminder that Divine love includes unconditional love for self as well as others.

XIII—Death

I t is said that death is the great equalizer, but no matter how evolved or spiritual one's perspective, when this card comes up in a reading, it can be intimidating. Here we sense that our current state of existence is about to radically change. The transformation implied in The Death card involves both a death and a rebirth. The first requires a willingness to let go of old ways of being, and the second, on a more hopeful note, being open to new experiences. I often refer to the Death card as The Wheel of Fortune Part Two because both cards focus on changing cycles. In The Wheel, it represented the evolution of one's karma through conscious choice. In Death, it is the growth that occurs through participation with the natural cycles of endings and new beginnings. Both cards emphasize the need to relinquish control as a part of the process.

On this path, it is important to remember that there are many kinds of death. This card may refer to the death of a relationship, the end of a career, or a time to let go of old behaviors that no longer serve you. One way or another, when Death appears, we must be willing to surrender to the process of transformation. Fighting our changes will only make things more difficult.

Some cultures embrace death more comfortably than others, just as some people may be more comfortable with the experiences of the Death card. A number of Eastern cultures, for example, see death as the supreme journey in transformation. In Western culture, we are less comfortable with death and may have the need for a crutch in our exploration of it. The current phenomenon of celebrity mediums, such as James Van Praagh and John Edwards, both with their own television shows, speaks to many people's desire to understand death and, more specifically, what happens afterward. Michael Newton, a hypnotist specializing in past life regression, has written a book on his experiences with various clients on this journey called *Journey of Souls*. Newton's work focuses on regressing people/souls to the point where they leave their body and their experience in the afterlife, what he describes as the journey of "life between lives." I recommend this book to clients who have lost loved ones or who are struggling with the meaning of death. Although his work may be a little out there to some, it reinforces the belief that death is just a beginning. The Death card represents endings, but also new beginnings. The transformation occurs in the journey between the two states.

Here are two stories that reflect different elements of the Death card. The first involves a friend and client, Angelica, who is a nurse and a hospice worker. She is often teased about her name, and many of her coworkers call her the "angel of death." Since her youth, Angelica has been fascinated with death, both as a spiritual journey and a physical process. As an adult, she felt called to work with people close to death. Angelica has often said that being with people at the moment of their passing was to her an extremely profound experience that she felt honored to be a part of. I would describe her as an old soul.

When she first started her career, she was greatly moved by her experience with a young man dying of AIDS. This was a few years back, before AIDS was commonly understood or accepted. Her patient had been an IV drug user and was tormented with guilt about his choices in life. Angelica felt that he needed to resolve these issues before his passing and encouraged him to explore his latent interest in spirituality. She provided him with different books that helped to give him a spiritual perspective about his journey in life and assisted in resolving much of his guilt. When he died, though she felt extremely sad, she was pleased for him in knowing that he had achieved some sense of peace. In the Death card, there is an opportunity for liberation regarding our choices in dealing with change. Sometimes this may mean needing to resolve old issues before we move on to our next experience.

Another expression of The Death card is reflected in the story of Linda, a marketing executive for a large software company. Linda lost her husband to cancer several years ago and at the time of her reading was still grieving. Her husband's form of cancer was both brutal and slow moving, and his death unfolded over a period of years, which had taken quite a toll on Linda. She had been in survival mode for so long that she had almost forgotten what a "normal" life was.

Her husband's death had greatly changed Linda. Because of it, people sometimes had a hard time relating to her and vice versa, and she was very cognizant of this. Those around her had not experienced the extremes she had and she felt that often she was, in her words, "too strong" for people. I find this extreme interpretation to be true of those with a Scorpio (Death's ruler) component to their astrology. Scorpio can be intense in nature. Those connected to this sign or the Death card are often very growth oriented. From a spiritual perspective, this could be described as the soul's desire to experience growth by creating different and sometimes difficult experiences in life in order to provide the opportunity for transformation. Obviously, when any death occurs, it is most often beyond our control. Yet on this path, we may need to look at the desire to cultivate, consciously and unconsciously, extreme experiences to facilitate growth. This can also be the case in the Judgment card (ruled by Pluto, the planet associated with Scorpio).

With those who have experienced many extremes in life, there can oftentimes be a sense of one constantly looking over one's shoulder waiting for the next bad thing to happen. This attitude not only interferes with the willingness to be open to new life, it also can taint the new experience. Linda was beginning to open herself up to a new relationship in her life and said she was scared that, because of her past experiences, she was going to be too much for him. She confided that one of her favorite songs was by Sheryl Crowe with the refrain, "Are you strong enough to be my man?" We talked about her need to relinquish control regarding this issue and to learn to trust the process. When I last heard from Linda, she and her new man were doing well together. She was learning to live again, which is one of the most important steps in the Death card.

As a child, one of my favorite holidays was Halloween. I spent a part of my childhood in Alabama, where the weather at the end of October was still warm enough that, when we went trick or treating, we could wear our costumes without coats or other encumbrances. This was liberating because it made the experience all the more real. I enjoyed all the hoopla around dressing up and getting candy (my favorite Halloween disguise was that of a gypsy fortune teller), but the part that intrigued me most was seeing witches, ghosts, and goblins for one magical evening milling about the neighborhood and giving it an otherworldly feel. Even as a child, I was interested in the occult, and to me, Halloween represented an opportunity to participate in mysterious elements outside of the normal parameters of my day-to-day existence.

This affinity reminds me of The Death card because here we experience unknown mysteries beyond our old parameters of knowing. I still enjoy Halloween, but as an adult, I have a more reverent attitude towards the occasion. Halloween, of course, comes from "All Hallow's Eve." In olden days, this night represented the time where souls passed on from their earthly existence into the next. In The Death card, we enter a journey of great change, often deeply transforming how we view ourselves and our experience of life. In Death, we can find life again, and it is the journey and what we choose to do with it that offers the opportunity for the most profound transformation.

XIV—Temperance

T emperance is a process of creative transformation that comes about through the integration of different elements in our life. Recently, I was reading a restaurant review for a new French bistro that had just opened in my neighborhood and was intrigued by the reviewer's description of the different ingredients in certain dishes and how they blended together to bring out the flavors in one another. His review reminded me of how I sometimes describe the Temperance card to my clients, using the analogy of a master chef combining different ingredients to come up with the perfect recipe. The Temperance card could be described as the process of creating a grand soup—the soup of life. For example, if you were to make minestrone, you would start with a broth, add chicken, pasta, some carrots, maybe onions, tomatoes, and potatoes. With only one ingredient, it would simply be tomato soup, or chicken, or potato. It is the combination and interaction of the different ingredients that creates something unique out of basic elements.

Gourmands are alchemists in the sense that they love to experiment with new and different ingredients. I have a client, a chef and a caterer, who is always preaching the power of experimentation in her work. She is frustrated by clients who are not willing to try something new, often bemoaning those who make safe choices and praising those willing to experiment. Temperance translates to the willingness to mix things up a bit and experiment with different elements and proportions in order to explore new dimensions in life. Different ingredients, whether in the form of new experiences, perceptions, knowledge, or insight, combine to bring us multi-dimensional wisdom.

TEMPERANCE.

Aleister Crowley called the Temperance card "Art." Crowley was referring to the art of learning, of gaining wisdom through intellectual and personal endeavor. This emphasizes learning through experience, which Crowley described as an art form. Just as a painter applies layer after layer of paint to a canvas until they achieve the perfect vision, we layer experience on experience toward the attainment of wisdom. The creative process combines the personality of the artist with a higher element of inspiration. The wisdom of Temperance comes from the integration of the human element with the Divine. Book knowledge can be helpful in understanding this process, but Temperance implies that the ultimate experience of wisdom comes from being the actual vessel for the experience. Which is to say: We become the canvas.

Jazz music is another art form that serves Crowley's theory well. Jazz is largely improvisational, and musicians often do not know what will happen from one moment to the next. This requires them to come together, in a sense to be at one with the music and other musicians, resulting in a sublime musical and creative harmony. Temperance, like jazz, could be described as a performance art that requires experimentation and the willingness to trust one's instincts. Legendary jazz musician Thelonious Monk was known for extreme experimentation. His work influenced many great jazz musicians to follow, helping to redefine not only his genre, but our ideas concerning others as well. Thelonious Monk was a musical alchemist, and he would probably describe his music as a transcendental art form.

The ancient art of alchemy involved combining different elements toward the ultimate goal of transforming lead into gold. The process of alchemy is both an art and a science. In ancient times, many alchemists considered themselves to be mystics and magicians. This element of magic reminds us of the Magician's path. As with The Magician's juggler, Temperance indicates the juggling of different elements or ingredients all at the same time. The key is in keeping all the balls in the air without becoming distracted. For example, on this path we often explore new and different life experiences, requiring us to shift from one to another and sometimes back again. This constant shifting and reorganization resembles the different stages of alchemy, with the end result being the right combination—gold itself. As in The Magician, this is a process of learning that requires discipline and focus.

In some extreme cases, Temperance may represent the interaction of too many different elements in one's life at the same time. Just as too many chefs spoil the broth, too many ingredients can result in chaos. Here we must trust our instincts concerning what needs to be weeded out and discarded to come up with the right balance.

Leonardo Da Vinci, one of greatest minds of all time, is an excellent example of both the creative and alchemical expressions of Temperance. Da Vinci was the original Renaissance man, combining art and science as a painter, sculptor, engineer, inventor, and scientist. Many of his inventions and theories anticipated the advances of modern science. Some of his greatest masterpieces, especially the *Mona Lisa*, are veiled in a cloud of mystery and secrecy, leading to the advent of conspiracy theories concerning his work. Perhaps in his art, Da Vinci was following the ancient tradition of secrecy employed by all mystics and by the ancient alchemists. These traditions are based on the idea that to discover true wisdom, one must be worthy of the process, a process of tests. Secrecy and mysticism go hand in hand, often as a way of protecting secrets from falling into the wrong hands.

The image of a grand angel, the Great Omnipresent Guardian Angel, fills the Temperance card. A guardian angel is a presence, often supernatural, that looks out for one's best interests: nudging us along in life, influencing, protecting, and saving us from harm. Angels have become very popular recently, with a variety of books written about them, specifically about individual experiences with them. While shopping for your Tarot deck, you may have seen the variety of Angel cards on the market. These decks are similar in concept to the Tarot, showing different angels and how their influence may work in our lives. My favorite is the popular little tiny deck of Angel cards. Each card is the size of a message that comes in a fortune cookie and includes only a single word: Integrity, Harmony, and Peace, to name a few. Their simplicity provides the opportunity to explore different applications and meanings, applying the higher mind in guiding one's interpretation, much like the guiding influence of a guardian angel.

The belief in guardian angels may come in different forms. For example, some people see them as heavenly guides or superior beings. You can find angels, in whatever form, everywhere in life. Some refer to people in their daily lives as "angels." I have heard many stories from clients describing how the right person came into their lives at the right moment to guide them on their way. In Temperance, it is important to be open to guidance, which may come in many different ways to instruct us on our path towards wisdom. The willingness to receive a higher influence in this journey can help awaken us to unlimited possibilities.

A modern day Renaissance man is Bill Gates, billionaire founder of the Microsoft Corporation. To some, Gates is an angel, especially in regard to his charitable and philanthropic work; to his critics, he is the devil himself. As *Fortune* magazine said, "Love him or hate him, but you can't ignore him." Whatever the view, Gates' groundbreaking innovations in the field of computer technology have done more to shape our present reality than anything in recent history. His company brought technology to the masses, enabling us to interact with knowledge in ways not possible before. In the tradition of Da Vinci, Gates is both inventor and entrepreneur, using science and the imagination to create a crucible for technological magic.

As one of the richest men in the world, he created the Bill and Melinda Gates Foundation, which funnels millions of dollars to worthy causes, including global health research, libraries, and most notably, schools. Through grants and technological support, his foundation has helped underprivileged students expand their opportunities to learn and grow in their own journeys towards wisdom. This combination of different ingredients—learning, technology, and generosity of spirit—is both a form of modern day alchemy and the Temperance card at its best.

XV—The Devil

In doing readings for clients from different backgrounds and belief systems, my experience is that the two cards that evoke the most extreme reaction universally are Death and The Devil. Both cards can be button-pushers, often bringing up fears around feeling out of control. There can be a superstitious element involved here, representing a belief that there are supernatural forces at work. In a sense, it is easy to understand where the fear comes from, as both images are frightening in appearance: Death with a skeleton in the form of the grim reaper and The Devil showing us a great hairy beast seemingly imprisoning two mortals in his chains of power. Yet just as Death rarely implies a physical death, The Devil even more rarely represents true evil. In fact, in my entire career, I have yet to see this as the case.

The simplest definition of The Devil card is fear; to me fear and The Devil are synonymous. In addition to fear, the key words for this card are power, control, and obsession. The Devil card represents an exploration of our dark side and one is sure to encounter at least one of these elements in the process. Here it may be helpful to define dark side. It is not an evil aspect of self. Instead, it could be described as a hidden part of self, like a dark closet full of secrets. It is our Pandora's box, the place where we hide unresolved issues, our unexplored fears and desires. It is also the place where the mystery of self and the universe comes from, and also where our deepest sexual nature and creative power lies.

THE DEVIL.

Everyone has a dark side, but some are more in touch with theirs than others. In the best sense, what The Devil shows us is that in facing the darkest elements of self, there can be liberation of the highest order. This card represents a time to make friends with your dark side, which may mean opening the closet of your secret self. Often this will require facing some of your deepest fears and the darker aspects of your nature. Here is a description of each key element of The Devil and how it may apply to your situation:

Control: We first met the devil in the form of a beast in the Strength card. Both paths represent an exploration of the inner-workings of our procreative (or life force) energy. Our passion and desires lie within this energy. Desire, like many aspects of The Devil card, is not inherently bad. In fact, just the opposite is often true, and when applied effectively, it can become one of the most powerful parts of self. Desire is the first step in any creative process and may come in different forms, depending on one's unique needs. Like its counterpart, procreative energy, desire is a very powerful force and at times may make one feel out of control. The key is in finding a way to channel and utilize this energy to your highest benefit.

In Vedic terms, this force of energy is called Kundalini, or the serpent power. In symbolism, the snake or serpent represents a test and a transformation. Here, the test is in learning to work with this energy, which is a process of transmutation. In Strength, we discovered that through a loving and patient exploration of our desire, we find the opportunity for self-transformation. Like the lion in Strength, if we try to cage or overtly control our passion, it can eat us up inside.

Obsession: The creative process is one form of exploring our dark side and people who relate to The Devil card often have strong creative natures. Yet, like anything, when out of balance, the creative process can turn into a form of obsession. Obsession could be described as a preoccupation with a persistent need or desire. When we enter the creative realm, it can be like entering a dark and unknown void. This can be both exhilarating and scary. Sometimes there is a fine line between creativity and addiction, where one can become addicted to both the highs and lows of the creative experience.

The danger lies in losing ourselves in this process. Some of the greatest minds in literature, Edgar Allen Poe or Lewis Carroll for example, had very strong dark sides and were bedeviled with addiction issues. This can be seen in other creative venues as well. The abstract artist Jackson Pollock or musician Janis Joplin are just two examples of the fine line between genius and self-destruction; ultimately both succumbed to their dark sides.

Sometimes when The Devil card comes up in a reading, it represents a time when we are obsessing about things outside of our control. In extreme cases, this may involve letting the mind run away to the point of losing touch with reality. The creative component of this card belies a strong sense of the imagination. When out of balance, it may conjure extreme scenarios—imagining the worst, for example. Often, this has little to do with the reality of the situation and obsessing will certainly only make things worse.

There is nothing more difficult than desiring something and, when it doesn't happen according to our plans, feeling severely let down. In these cases, learning to surrender to a higher system may help to remedy the situation.

Power: The ruler for The Devil card is Capricorn and, in the best sense, this sign represents responsible power and authority. In the previous Arcanum, Temperance, we looked at the possible misuse of wisdom. The Devil can similarly represent the misuse of power. Again, power in itself is not bad: We all have a need to feel powerful in our lives and this is a good thing, it's what we do with it that is important. The dark side of power can be in the need to manipulate others to get what we want. This may come in the form of power for the sake of power, which is often ego-based. Throughout history, there are many examples of this: leaders in power who misuse their authority for their own means, often taking advantage of others in the process. This can be seen in various political, religious, and business arenas, but we may find ourselves in this situation in our day-to-day lives as well. Often The Devil card represents power struggles in relationships. Here we must take ownership of our role in helping to create this.

The need to feel powerful can sometimes relate to the need to feel secure by the attainment of material goods. This could be described as trophy collecting, where the more trophies or possessions we have, the greater we feel. This is false power. The Devil card can represent a time to look at your materialist needs to see if they are out of balance.

What follows is an interesting and somewhat unique case study on the inner-workings of The Devil card. Stephanie is a client who, in middle age, became fascinated with religion and spirituality, completing a master's degree in theology. She was beginning to teach classes in applying spiritual truths in everyday life, and the response was overwhelmingly successful. For example, several different church groups had asked her to come in and teach workshops, and some business associations had even approached her for her services. Yet she was hesitant. We did a reading on this matter, and The Devil card showed up. I was intrigued because Stephanie seemed to be on the right path, and I was curious to see how The Devil would fit into her scenario.

Stephanie then related this story. Several years ago, she had gone to see a hypnotist who specialized in past life regression. A past life where she had been a major church leader in power during the dark period of the European Inquisitions came up in her session. In this lifetime, she had greatly misused her religious authority, which led to the deaths of many innocent people.

Stephanie said this aligned with a vivid and recurring dream she'd had since young adulthood of herself as a stout gray-haired man wearing the robes of a bishop. In these dreams, she found herself experiencing, as if for real, what seemed to be the witch hunt trials of the Inquisition. Stephanie was overwhelmed by the connection between her regression experience and her dream. She wasn't sure whether this was a past life memory, but the end result was a deep fear of misusing her spiritual authority in this lifetime.

Stephanie is a closet bisexual often troubled with guilt about her attraction to women. She sometimes wondered if her sexual preferences were influenced by this possible past life as a man. This led to confusion about her sexuality and inhibited her freedom in expressing her true needs.

I have read for Stephanie for many years, and I would say she carries an essence of goodness. We discussed that, with her innate integrity, it would be unlikely for her to mislead others. This would be against her nature. There could also be a possibility that cosmically, in this lifetime, she was being given an opportunity to right the wrongs of the past, not in the sense of wrongdoings on her part, but more as a part of a grander scheme. We also discussed that she needed to accept her sexual preferences and stop judging herself.

Her story receives emphasis here because it reflects additional elements of The Devil card: guilt, self-judgment, and secret shame. Stephanie has now put the past behind her and is bravely plowing forward in her spiritual work. She is beginning to embrace its importance, especially in regards to helping others to feel more powerful in their spiritual journeys. In the process, she is conquering her fears and discovering her own true power.

If we ignore our dark side—or worse, stuff it away—we give it the power to control us. The ultimate lesson in The Devil is that only in facing our dark sides can we regain a sense of empowerment. We must confront what we fear in order to heal ourselves.

XVI—The Tower

September 11, 2001. When the disastrous occurrences of this infamous day happened, I was, like most people were, glued to CNN and the entire media onslaught that was available. As I watched the footage of the planes striking the World Trade Center, beyond the feeling of shock and disbelief, something kept tugging at my brain—a feeling of familiarity. Then I realized, "My God! This is The Tower card." The image of The Tower card, originating in antiquity, is almost like a medieval snapshot of the actual event that happened in New York City on 9/11. Instead of a bolt of lightening, planes were destroying the towers, and innocent people were literally falling to their deaths.

The Tower card had become all too real. In a flash of lightning, our consciousness was changed, and the world would never be the same again. For some time, a few years at least, I had been seeing a predominance of The Tower card showing up in readings. This was perhaps a precursor of what was to come. Yet the unfathomable reality, the world's grief for the victims and their families, is something no one could ever be prepared for.

A time of major world transition has been predicted throughout history. The new millennium brought many apocalyptic predictions. The 14th century French mystic and prophet Nostradamus, and his cryptic poems about world destruction, serve as one example. The visions that Nostradamus put into words are fascinating in their seeming accuracy. There are many online chat rooms and websites dedicated to deciphering his poems and their deep meanings. The end of the Mayan calendar has created similar discussion about "the end of the world." Whether metaphoric or real, it is important to remember that many of these prophecies have yet to play out or come into being.

To astrologers, this time on our planet represents the shift in ages that occurs every 2,000 years. Now we are entering into the Age of Aquarius, a time that offers the hope of eventual world peace and the brotherhood of humankind. Ultimately, this is a time of promise for the beginning of spiritual unity on earth.

All of these predictions suggest that destruction, in some form or another, will be a part of the process. So in a way what is happening in the world is somewhat inevitable. Of course choice and free will play into how this will take place. Nothing is set in stone at this moment. Many believe that this cycle of extreme transformation is a transitional process, a process that will take place for years to come and will not be over anytime soon.

In the world there is what is known as the microcosm (representing self) and the macrocosm (representing the collective), meaning that the chaotic events happening in the world were being reflected in people's individual lives—as above, so below. In working with clients during this extreme period, whether it was in their work, or relationships, or general well-being, people were towering in one way or another. By towering I mean experiencing a general feeling of helplessness or not being in control. For some, it was a feeling of self-destructing. The most common theme was a desire for life to get back to normal—as quickly as possible.

The Tower represents external death, and I was watching clients go through their own processes and stages of death: denial, anger, bargaining, and ultimately acceptance. What The Tower card tells us is that there is no going backward, only forward, and that by acknowledging the death (or change) it will be easier for the rebirth to begin. Transformation is a process of both death and rebirth; you cannot have one without the other.

Mars (ruler of The Tower) is an aggressive planet and is often described by astrologers as a malevolent force, meaning that this is a time to exercise caution, to be mindful about not putting yourself in dangerous situations or at risk. There could be unforeseen forces at work and you don't want to get in the way, otherwise you may court disaster. Let the situation work itself through, then you can reengage.

To explore your Tower more deeply, do a reading for yourself using the Moon Spread. This will help to give you a sense of where you are coming from and where you are going.

Stories are history come alive in a way that stimulates the imagination to possible new beginnings. J.R.R. Tolkein and his epic, *The Lord of the Rings,* and the phenomenon of *Harry Potter* by J.K. Rowling both serve as good examples of this. Both authors are gifted storytellers, mystics even, tapped into a collective fable that must be told. What their stories share in common is the theme of good versus evil where the fate of humanity is at stake. Watching *The Lord of the Rings* movies can be a cathartic experience. We laugh, cry, and cheer. We don't feel so alone in our own day-to-day struggles. Claudia Puig (of *USA Today*) said this about the series: "The films tell a classic story that espouses the virtues of love, hard work, and compassion and decries greed, deceit, and the abuse of power in a mighty struggle against the temptation and corrupting forces of power." Tolkien created this story during World War II, an epic struggle between the forces of good and evil. It mirrors the events occurring in our world today and gives us a timeless context to the topography of evil.

Now is a time where science fiction is becoming reality. Even though the Harry Potter stories are based in fantasy, there are parallels to Harry's magical journey and what is happening in the world today. There are also some interesting similarities between the events in Harry's world and The Tower card. For example, the image of the Phoenix figures prominently in the Harry Potter stories.

Harry is a boy-wizard who has experienced death first hand—that of his parents and nearly himself—and survived. In the wizarding community, he is known as "the boy who lived." He has the scar to prove it: a bolt of lightening enblazoned on his forehead. Aficionados of Harry's story know that his magic wand is made from the tail feather of a Phoenix. When Harry fights evil-incarnate, the Lord Voldemort, and is bit by a serpent's poisonous fangs, it is this magical bird that brings him back to life through the healing power of its tears.

Harry Potter's evil nemesis, Lord Voldemort, is referred to as "he-who-must-not-be-named." In Kabalistic teachings, The Tower is represented by the letter "Peh," meaning mouth, which can be related to speech. The parable of the Tower of Babel has much to do with speech and language. Words have power. Robert Wang, in his book, *The Qabalistic Tarot* says: "Properly vibrated with Martian force, they help to bring about the destruction of our personal towers, false concepts, and institutions which we believe to be reality." Unlike his contemporaries, Harry Potter was willing to name Voldemort, thus diminishing the evil lord's power. In The Tower, we conquer our fears of the unknown, which sometimes means standing up against our adversaries and those who oppose what we believe in—our personal truths.

Harry Potter, like The Tower, reminds us that when good is pitted against evil, good will ultimately triumph and live. In these turbulent times, we must believe in magic, in something bigger than ourselves and in the possible miracle of transformation. We can make a difference, no matter how big or small.

XVII—The Star

he Star is the first of the Luminaries of the Tarot. Astrologer Liz Greene, in her book *The Luminaries*, refers to the traditional definition of a Luminary as "a source of light," and, "one who illustrates any subject or instructs humankind." She further describes the quality of a Luminary as "a personal standard of excellence in body, heart and mind, and our personal models of the best that might be achieved." The Star has the potential to influence the destiny of others. Stars have the ability to connect to a bigger picture and are often vessels of a higher order. If you have chosen this card, it is a reminder, an affirmation, to you that whether in big or small ways, you do indeed make a difference.

When I think about the essence of The Star what comes to mind is the image of Martin Luther King giving his famous "I have a dream" speech. His powerful presence, filled with passionate and righteous indignation regarding the nation's state of affairs, inspired his audience to believe in, to dare to imagine, a different future where

THE STAR.

every human race is equal. His message is unforgettable and as relevant today as it was in the 1960s—perhaps even more so.

Stars are often visionaries, as was King. He set the standard of unlimited possibilities for the nation and the world. King's vision is an Aquarian one: world unity and the brotherhood of humankind. It is an interesting coincidence that our national Martin Luther King Day usually falls on the first day of Aquarius, January 21st.

Greene quotes Carl Jung, in regards to the Luminaries, in saying, "if there is something wrong with society, there is something wrong with the individual; and if there is something wrong with the individual, there is something wrong with me." This means that we are all tied to one anther and to the outcomes we as individuals and as a collective create. The Star reminds us that the individual consciousness defines what is and will be the universal consciousness and vice versa: As above, so below.

The Star has much to do with the imagination, especially in regards to being able to imagine a different future for others and ourselves. The fallen Beatle John Lennon and his musical prayer for world peace, "Imagine," illustrate this concept brilliantly. In light of the disastrous occurrences of September 11th his words seem especially prophetic: "Imagine there's no country, it isn't hard to do. Nothing to kill or die for and no religion too. Imagine all the people living life in peace. You may say I'm a dreamer… I hope some day you'll join us, and the world will be as one."

Lennon was stimulated by personal dissatisfaction with his life, and the world in general. Ultimately, his dissatisfaction became inspiration, resulting in a prolific creative output. Lennon was ahead of his time and, though he saw himself as sometimes persecuted by our government because of it, he embraced America and especially New York, calling both his home.

Many of us remember exactly what we were doing the moments that President John F. Kennedy, Martin Luther King, and John Lennon were shot. Their deaths represented the end of an era for most of us. But, as with all Luminaries, their lights shine on.

Now there is a whole new generation of Stars keeping the dream alive. A prime example lies in the band Pearl Jam, part of the musical "grunge" movement that originated in Seattle in the early 1990s. This band represents the largesse of spirit of The Star. They have been a constant proponent of equality for women and have given many free performances for charity. They illustrate creative expression in alignment with a greater good. The whole wave of the "grunge" movement represented a new order in music. These were musical revolutionaries defying the establishment for a less commercial approach to their art. Music is a reflection of what is going on in the universal consciousness. Music, poetry, literature, and visual art are all creative expressions that define our times.

Maybe you remember the song "The Dawning of the Age of Aquarius" with its lyrics, "When the Moon is in the seventh house and Jupiter aligns with Mars, then peace will guide the planets and love will steer the stars." It may sound corny now but there is a basis for its being. This song came as a result of the revolutionary 1960s, a period where the clamor for civil rights reached a crescendo, a time where the concept of free love was being embraced and explored again.

The Age of Aquarius represents a coming unity—the brotherhood of humankind. The Tower, the previous Arcanum and the path of destruction, began to clear the way for this rebirth. This is and will be an ongoing creative process. There is no standard for what comes next because we have never been here before.

The Age of Aquarius is a balance between the personal and the universal. In astrology, the Age of Aquarius is symbolized as the polarity between the signs Leo (the Lion) and Aquarius (the Cosmic Water-Bearer). Leo represents personal, creative, self-expression. Aquarius represents the cosmic or universal expression of a bigger consciousness. The Age of Aquarius is a symbol for the coming together of the two in a harmonious way.

A practical example lies in the way that the work environment has evolved. Now more than ever, work is less about punching a time clock and more about doing something fulfilling. Today, it is not unusual for someone to work at home, independent but a part of a bigger whole. It is about life fitting the needs of the individual and thus better serving the collective. The older structures of commerce are fast becoming obsolete and many corporations, as they seek new ways to restructure, are keeping the needs of the individual in mind. This symbiotic relationship between the organization and the individual holds untold possibilities. By being willing to reinvent ourselves in keeping with the times, to be creative about the structure of our day to day lives, there is success of a whole new order at hand. Now more than ever, change is the name of the game.

Oprah Winfrey, an Aquarius, is another example of a current-day Star. As Winfrey has shared her personal journey of growth and enlightenment, she often cites various Luminaries who have personally inspired her. Remember the time before Oprah was a household word? She has brilliantly used the media to present options for change in an individual life. Her popularity is due to her ability to tap into what the collective needs, whether it be therapy, spirituality, or shopping and makeover tips. Oprah was one of the first talk show hosts who embraced exploring one's intuition and deeper emotions in a dignified way. Oprah represents a media phenomenon. By acknowledging individuals, the everyday people with their journeys and experiences, she gives them a means to change their lives.

The Star is creative light, representing a potential within us all to create and define our futures. Author and creative writing teacher Brenda Ueland, author of *If You Want to Write*, begins the first chapter in her book with, "Everybody is talented, original, and has something important to say." Her message, that everyone's aspirations are worthwhile, applies not only to writers, but all creative people. Her book, first published in the 1930s, was so relevant, it was reprinted through the 1980s. I found a copy of it many years ago, or rather the book found me, at a time when I was considering a career as a professional writer. It literally fell off a bookstore shelf at my feet, and I have relied on its wisdom for years.

Ueland's book has given timeless inspiration to many writers. She herself was inspired by Blake and quotes him as saying, "Imagination is the divine body in every man." She describes the creative power, the imagination, as the Holy Ghost: "It is the spirit. In fact it is the only important thing about us." Another of her chapters is entitled: "Be careless, Reckless! Be a lion! Be a pirate! When you write." On the path of The Star, we must become lions of the new order and boldly use our creative power of imagination to write a different future.

It is not unusual for Stars to be greatly influenced by a universal or cosmic consciousness, meaning that your ideas are most probably in sync with a higher order. The Star card is like a cosmic blessing, a green light and a big thumbs-up to you regarding your new endeavors. Granted, on this path, there are no pre-determined outcomes, but by taking a risk and following your inspiration, there will definitely be a positive change in your future.

XVIII—The Moon

he Moon card rules the subconscious. When it comes up in a reading, it can indicate the need for some deep inner-work to resolve unfinished business, especially of an emotional or spiritual nature. The Moon's shadow can be a disease in one's innermost being or soul, which can lead to a spiritual crisis. In Egyptian mythology, the moon symbolizes the receptacle of souls between incarnations. The Moon represents a time to let go of the past, whether from this lifetime or another, and move onto new experiences. It foreshadows the rebirth that lies ahead in The Sun card.

I often refer to The Moon as the "Therapy Card," meaning that, when it shows up, it may portend a time to check in with a professional for some fine-tuning of your psyche to bring it into a state of harmony. An analogy would be a car, representing the vehicle or chariot for your soul. Every 3,000 miles (or years or days) a tune-up is in order. You employ a professional to clean out the stuck "oil" that interferes with optimum performance, here representing your psyche's ability to function in full health.

THE MOON.

It is so important to not isolate one's self on this path. Instead, ask for help from someone who can give you a detached perspective of your process. It can make all the difference in your dark night of the soul—to go from feeling frustrated and overwhelmed to beginning a healing journey.

Those with an affiliation to The Moon card are often greatly affected by the moon's cycles, especially the full moon. In Astrology, those with a strong emphasis in the Water signs (Cancer, Scorpio, and Pisces) are usually most influenced, but this can apply to everyone. The moon's cycles affect the earth, for example, in the gravitational pull of the ocean tides. When the moon is full, it is often standard practice for hospitals and the police force to put on extra personnel to deal with the lunar fallout. The word lunacy comes from lunar. Empirical data tells us that the moon greatly affects our moods and even our psychological function. Our planet has been in an intense eclipse cycle of both the sun and the moon. Eclipses represent big changes, transformations, especially of a karmic nature. This applies both to the planet as a whole and also the individual self. This card instructs us to pay attention to the influence of the moon and how it affects your life.

The Moon card is often attributed with a releasing of old karma. The word karma comes from the Hindu Goddess Kali Ma, the Goddess of Creation and Destruction. Kali is known as "The Dark Mother." The moon, as a symbol for the feminine and cycles, is often closely associated with women. Menstrual cycles represent a time when a woman was considered to be her most powerful. In ancient times, the full moon was seen as a time to journey within, to embrace one's darkness. It was thought that by doing so, one connected to inner power. The Native American tradition of sweat lodges and vision quests embraces this concept, also called a shamanic death.

One of my Tarot friends (we hang out, pull some cards, and get the general psychic forecast of what is ahead) once confessed to me, "Of all the cards I most dread, it is The Moon." This was interesting because most people react to the Death or The Devil cards in this way, with a feeling of fear. When I asked why, she answered, "Because The Moon is so confusing." Going into the unknown can be both scary and confusing. Emotions and intuitions—the realm of The Moon—do not always line up in a linear manner. This may manifest itself as a feeling of being out of control. The Moon card is often described as representing a process of necessary madness. Exploring your darkness, the deepest reaches of your psyche, can make one feel a bit "mad."

In the Medicine Cards, a deck of Native American animal totems by Jamie Sams and David Carson, the Wolf is described as a teacher and a pathfinder, saying that, "The senses of Wolf are very keen, and the moon is its power ally. The moon is the symbol of psychic energy, or the unconscious that holds the secrets of knowledge and wisdom." They describe Wolf "medicine" as empowering "the teacher within us all to come forth and aid the children of Earth in understanding the Great Mystery and life." The word Arcana is Latin for secrets or mystery, and the Tarot offers a journey into your own mystery. The wolf appears in The Moon card to point the way to the wisdom that lies in darkness.

The Wolf is a part of "the pack," the universal family, and also a solitary nomad, embodying individual dreams and ideas. This idea aligns well with the concept of a Luminary: The Moon is reflected light and represents our ability to reflect back to others (the pack) what can be learned on our own individual journey in life.

The planetary ruler for Pisces is Neptune, the mythological God of the Sea. Neptune represents water without boundaries. Imagine a huge ocean where all things flow together as one, or a glass of water without the container. The element of Water often brings up merging issues: the often unconscious ability to absorb or get caught up in other people's lives. This is a psychic process because it relates to the non-physical realm.

Mary Ann's story serves a prime example of a psychic merging. She was a client who came to me experiencing depression and a profound sense of hopelessness. The Moon card figured prominently in Mary Ann's reading. As it turns out, her mother was stricken with Alzheimer's disease, and death for her had become a turbulent and unsettling process. I say turbulent because Mary Ann's mother had unresolved issues that were holding her back from releasing the past and moving on to the next stage of her journey. What came up in Mary Ann's reading was that she had psychically and emotionally merged with her mother and had taken on her depression. By setting clear boundaries—a process of separation—she got her sense of self back and was able to be there for her mother in her time of need without taking on her struggle.

A healthy Moon has good boundaries. When out of balance, The Moon can be a recipe for codependence or addictive behavior. On this path, we are encouraged to work on our boundaries. This especially applies to your relationships with family, friends, and partners. This is a time to get clear about where you start and others end.

The opening from a poem by Claudia Mauro, a gifted poet, writer, and teacher, illustrates the many aspects of The Moon card. She has inspired many writers to explore their darkness as a part of the creative process. Claudia also has much personal experience with the inner workings of addiction recovery. To me, her poem represents an addiction to longing for dreams—although beautiful and romantic—that haven't been fulfilled.

This Is the Poem I Can Never Show You

A promise to control the tide, is always a lie.

The resolute moon, is more persistent than the best
of intentions.

The simple truth is that, when you speak, the wind
stills.

I watch your mouth move—words float by half heard
and buzz against my skin. When you laugh, the
ceiling cracks and the sky arcs open impossibly blue.

When I dream, you curl around the edge, of my
wishes and vanish soft as a whispered prayer, an
opening eye.

Now I live by the ocean, which is a good place to cry.

A woman wants to feel, like she's filling something as
she watches, a dream fade into daylight, like a star.

There is a phenomenon I call psychic dating. Simply put, it is where we have a relationship with someone that is not necessarily reflected in the physical world. The connection is more in our imaginations. Imagination and the psyche go hand in hand and this can be dangerous ground, representing the possibility for getting caught in illusions. Pisces can represent unrequited love.

One of the best descriptions of The Moon/Pisces I have heard is that they have an innate homesickness, a constant remembering of what it is like to swim in the universal womb or ocean. Pisces is the last sign of the Zodiac. It symbolizes the step where the soul merges back with Source, becoming one again. Thus, the process of incarnating may lead to a sense of separation anxiety. Moon/Pisces often seeks transcendental experiences as a way of feeling connected or transcending the body to symbolically remerge. At its worst, addiction can be a part of the peril but, if channeled creatively, the result may be some of our most powerful work.

XIX—The Sun

The Sun card represents those who are bright lights and whose presence inspires us to believe in positive outcomes. Those who identify with this card tend to be creative individuals with a desire to share their gifts with others as a form of self-expression. Suns are optimists. For them, the proverbial cup is most always half full. We find Suns everywhere. They are not just lofty individuals in power, although The Sun's bright light may lead to fame, but can just as well be the person at the checkout counter at your local Safeway. They shine a little of their light our way and somehow we feel better just by their acknowledging our presence. Their graciousness is like a sprinkling of gold dust and provides some needed relief to what may be an otherwise dreary day.

The Dalai Lama of Tibet personifies the bright and joyful essence of The Sun card. A great spiritual leader, he has experienced unthinkable tragedy and persecution and has persevered. Even with the gravity of his situation, he seems to maintain a positive attitude about the

possibility for world change, never losing hope for eventual enlightenment on our planet. Those who have had the immense pleasure of an audience with his eminence often speak of his childlike nature, remarking that he is filled with humor and is often found giggling. The Dalai Lama is the embodiment of Divine Child. He emits light—a lightness of being—and it is said that by being in his presence, one is transformed. His Sun-like innocence combines with a worldly wisdom creating a spiritual leader who is human and easy to relate to, and at the same time, connected to a bigger spiritual picture. He has the ability to embrace the human condition without judgment. He is not a reactionary but a gracious revolutionary.

Suns like the Dalai Lama are magnetic and powerful. For example, much like transforming lead into gold, he has been able attract others to his cause by directing his will towards positive outcomes.

His is a meditation on the power of positive thought: that by taking one day at a time, anything is possible. If you have chosen The Sun card, then your own light is igniting and leading you to the potential for a bigger and brighter existence.

Maggie, a healer and one of my clients, is another example of The Sun card. Maggie always believes in the highest potential for her friends and clients. She casts a very bright light and has a strong ego in the sense that she genuinely believes in her ability to help and heal others. She has an abundance of energy and tends to energize others. Maggie is a positive force of nature, and through thick and thin, she embraces all possibilities for herself and others. She has an almost child-like innocence, which works both for and against her. Her belief in all possibilities sometimes leads to disappointment when those around her don't reach what she believes to be their highest potential.

Maggie has experienced great personal tragedy in her young life. She lost people close to her in accidents and even in self-inflicted deaths. She felt like she was surrounded by death, and often experienced guilt about not being able to save those closest to her. Maggie was burnt-out and exhausted. She couldn't be Super Healer all the time.

The Sun's bright energy may burn itself out. The Sun is a universal symbol representing vitality which, when over-extended, can get tapped out. The Sun card mirrors the planetary sun, which is a power source, and like an energetic generator, when its circuits become overloaded, the result can be a blackout. Maggie needed to take time to recharge her batteries. As she experienced her own dark night of the soul—The Moon card—she learned about boundaries both for herself and for others.

Maggie is now in a process of rebirth. It is time for her to be selfish—self-full—and focus on her own needs instead of thinking she always needs to help others. It is time for her to live and let live. In the process, she is experiencing her own vulnerabilities, parts of herself that she has buried deep inside. Maggie is regaining her strength by healing her own emotional issues.

Another of my clients, Valerie, was a struggling actress stuck in a continual process of auditions and callbacks. She was becoming discouraged and felt like she was on a constant treadmill of rejection. Tired of hearing that she wasn't the right "type," she had worked hard to lose weight and her self-esteem suffered as a result of the pressure. She was perpetually worrying about being too aggressive and stepping on toes, yet wanting others to see her and craving recognition for her talents. This was especially true in her relationship with her agent. Valerie felt like her agent ignored her, but was hesitant about being too pushy. She felt like she would never achieve the success she had worked for and was on the verge of throwing in the towel.

During Valerie's reading, The Sun card indicated that her individuality was actually the key to her success. We discussed the need to assert herself, that by standing out, not "fitting in," she would finally earn the recognition she deserved. In the process, Valerie needed to take back her power and be who she was—to shine, to be bright—without worrying so much about how she was received by others. This idea liberated her and gave her the confidence necessary to finally achieve her goals.

The Sun represents success, which is sometimes difficult for people to adjust to. This is especially true for those who have experienced hardship in their lives. It requires a shift in consciousness. The Sun represents our vital essence, which is compromised when we worry, taking away our power and strength. On this path, we find that by letting go of worry and stress, we experience a burst of energy, like a solar flare, opening us to more creative expression. The motto for The Sun card is Carpe Diem, meaning "seize the day." Here we seize the day and make it our own.

Creative visualization can be a helpful tool in achieving success. For example, if you are experiencing a difficult situation, visualize a positive outcome. By being able to see what you desire in your mind's eye, it can become real.

The Sun brings the freedom to express oneself: positive self-expression and the need to be selfish in a balanced way. Suns tend to be catalysts. However, like a bright light that shines in the window, sometimes the light can be overbearing and we just want to pull down the shade. In some cases, as in the story of Icarus, we can fly too close to the sun. In mythology, Icarus was the great inventor who made wings to fly to the sun. If he flew too high, his wax wings would melt. Icarus defied his father's wishes, in what could be described as youthful impetuousness or arrogance, and soared to the sun anyway. We all know the end of the story. He had to fall. As always, it's a matter of balance. When The Sun is out of balance, one can have too much false ego and feel too important for the wrong reasons. The other cards in your spread can help to indicate whether this applies to you. Here it may be helpful to use the Destiny Spread (see page 30).

XX—Judgment

here are three "death" cards in the Tarot's Major Arcana: Death, The Tower, and Judgment. All represent extreme transformation through a process of death and rebirth. Yet Judgment is somewhat different from its counterparts because it focuses specifically on rebirth, the key to this card.

The best example I can give you of The Judgment card is my own process. While writing on it, I reinjured my back. This had me in bed, flat on my back. I couldn't move, walk, or work. The result was that I felt totally and completely helpless. With a lot of time on my hands, I was left to contemplate my whole life. I had to realize that I had not been taking care of myself. The combination of working too much and a program of strenuous exercise had me out of sync with my body and by being. This was not the first time my back went out when I was stressed. What I have found with clients experiencing this card is that they often put themselves in an extreme position of having to make changes. Now I was one of them.

JUDGEMENT.

At that point, I had already realized that, while working on this book, I was experiencing the essence of each Arcanum—I found that my life embodied the meaning of each card. This journey had me charting all the emotions one could think of.

Originally, I began this card with a line from the poem "Resurrection Day" by Rumi: "On Resurrection Day, God will say, 'What did you do with the strength and the energy your food gave you on Earth?'" The poem continues with one question after another. The questions of which Rumi speaks are: "What have you done with your entire life?" You might consider checking out and reading this poem in its entirety, as there is intensity to this card that is reflected in Rumi's work.

As in the poem, I was reviewing my whole life, and was in a state of despair. Then another line from Rumi's poem began to resonate in my head: "Prayer is an egg. Hatch out the total helplessness inside." I was focusing on everything that was wrong instead of the opportunity to make change. It was then that it dawned on me, like Michael's trumpet blaring in my head. "It's the rebirth, dummy!" It was time for my own resurrection.

As a result of my condition, I was forced to deal with my body. My psychic nature has not always made me feel comfortable in the physical realm. For a few days, I was in a state of denial, but ultimately, the pain of my injury got to me and I finally saw a chiropractor. The chiropractor, a kind and caring man, pointed out to me that my family history of back problems did not have to become mine, that I could change it. After many visits, and physical therapy, I started taking yoga classes. At first I felt like an idiot. I could barely touch my toes, let alone do a downward dog. Yet I never felt judgment from the other participants in the class, even though they were much more practiced than me. The teacher stressed that in the discipline of Yoga, ignorance is the path towards consciousness and we are not to judge. I felt like he was talking to me, saying that it was okay to be there and to take it one step at a time. In my own process of healing, I became much less judgmental towards others.

Also, because I wasn't able to work much during this time, I had to get very clear about my financial picture. This involved dealing with the reality of my day-to-day monies, again an area of my life I have not always been comfortable with. Scorpio, the sign of the Zodiac ruled by Pluto, is a "money" sign that is often expressed in one of two ways: either too much attention to material needs or not enough. I fell into the latter category, and now I needed to take brave step. I decided to do a budget, forcing me to become accountable for my spending habits. All of these changes led me to experience my life, my body as well as my finances, with a renewed vigor and sense of purpose. Whereas the glass had been half empty, now it was half full. As synchronicity with the Judgment card would have it, the situation forced me to make changes that I needed to make. I did indeed feel reborn.

Writer and poet Maya Angelou, author of *I Know Why the Caged Bird Sings,* has been quoted as saying, "Know better—do better." Her story sets an example for those of us on the path of Judgment.

Angelou has said there are many aspects of her life she is not proud of, yet she accepts her journey. She has said that if, at the end of the day, she is okay with God, then she is okay with herself. She imparts the timeless wisdom that if you have not walked in the shoes of another, you cannot judge their actions.

When Judgment appears in a reading, it represents the need for attention to an aspect of your life that requires transformation. Whatever the situation, there is usually a test involved. This path represents facing your truth and the reality of your life—and the willingness to act on it accordingly. In the end, forgiveness is the key to redemption in all matters. The act of self-acceptance is essential to this path.

Robert, one of my clients, came for a reading at an extreme moment in his life. He was considering leaving a marriage that had gone sour, and he didn't want to deal with the situation. Because of his disillusionment with the marriage, Robert had begun an affair. For most of his adult life, Robert had flirted with a drinking problem, and now it was quickly becoming serious. His finances were in disarray, and he needed to take charge or he would be forced to declare bankruptcy. He knew that he was at a turning point, and he felt guilty about his inability to make change. Overwhelmed by everything, he was avoiding dealing with himself.

It was no surprise that The Judgment card showed up in his reading. It was also joined by The Devil card, representing fear-based behaviors and a giving in to his dark side. This was a double whammy, signaling the need for conscious attention to his life, but at that time, Robert was not ready to make changes and he left the reading feeling frustrated. I was concerned for him, but knew from personal experience that one cannot make changes until they are truly ready. I wished him well.

About six months later, Robert came for another reading. He looked totally different. He had lost weight and seemed very vulnerable, yet exuded a newfound strength. Robert told me he had been in a minor car accident and had gotten a DUI. This was a wake-up call and forced him to get clear about his life. During his court proceedings, he was encouraged to go to AA. The supportive and non-judgmental atmosphere of the group allowed him to express his feelings, which was a cathartic experience. Robert had decided to leave both his marriage and the affair and spend more time with himself to figure out what was best for him. His was a baptism by fire, but he said he was now grateful for his experiences as they stimulated him to make the changes necessary to his growth.

In this reading, The Judgment card came up again, but this time it was joined by The Sun. This combination was an affirmation to him that he had gained the necessary wisdom to embark on a new journey in life and that he was truly on a path of rebirth. He felt encouraged and left this reading with a smile knowing that he was on the right path.

These stories are extreme examples of The Judgment card and serve as a reminder that you don't have to get to an extreme point in your life in order to make changes. Judgment's ruler Pluto represents the soul's desire for growth. Often those with a strong Pluto or Scorpio emphasis in their astrological makeup tend to unconsciously strive for growth at all costs. Ultimately, a part of the evolution for these types is learning to grow without crisis. With consciousness and attention, you can achieve rebirth without experiencing extreme crisis.. On this path, healing comes from compassionate acceptance for yourself and your process. By embracing change with heart and soul, and recognition for the human condition, transformation can happen in a way you never dreamed possible.

XXI—The World

In the World card, we realize that each of us are individually responsible for creating our reality and the world that we live in. How we participant with energy, both on a physical/personal and universal level, is an important part of this process. Medical intuitive Carolyn Myss, in her popular book, *Anatomy of the Spirit: The Seven Stages of Power and Healing,* underscores this idea, stating, "Everything that is alive pulsates with energy and all of this energy contains information." Her pioneering work with "energy medicine," and how personal and individual energy defines physical health, has changed the way modern medicine sees healing. Myss believes the emotional energy created by life experiences is reflected in our physical energy field. Myss says, "In this way, your biography—that is, the experiences that make up your life—becomes your biology." These are important ideas to The World's path as we become empowered to create successful and productive lives.

The concept that the human body is a vessel of energy became graphically real to me when I decided to visit a psychic surgeon, Dr.

THE WORLD.

Alex from the Philippines. I was skeptical, but he had a reputation for being a miracle worker. Several clients and friends I respect had experienced his supposedly amazing ability to heal and had resolved some of their trickiest physical maladies. But the biggest selling point was that he was Shirley MacLaine's psychic surgeon, a healer to the stars. Admittedly, I was intrigued. That and what did I have to lose? Well, as it happens, about $200, and this was several years ago. Dr. Alex's healing abilities did not come cheap.

Setting up a session with Dr. Alex consisted of receiving a map in the mail with an appointed date and time and directions to a secret location. Upon arrival, I noticed cars parked around the block and people streaming in. From the size of the crowd one would have thought there was a stadium event going on. We had to fill out release forms and describe three physical issues that we wanted Dr. Alex to address. Then we got into a long line that serpentined through the house and waited. There were many believers and much whispering about his magical touch. Some were seriously ill and I felt humbled, being in relatively good health. At the same time, I was turned off by what seemed to be a cult following.

Dr. Alex appeared to be a simple, unpretentious man beaming with sincerity. He explained that in his country, there was no need to prove how he worked, but in America we needed to see to believe. A demonstration was in order. An audience member was selected and I watched in awe and disbelief as Dr. Alex put his hand through the surface of the participant's skin. Then drawing out his hand, he placed several bloody polyps into a pan. There were gasps all around. How was this possible? Was this a trick of the mind? I had visceral shock and almost passed out.

When my turn came, I got onto the table, but couldn't watch. Then came what was the strangest sensation I have ever experienced—I could actually feel his hand moving inside my body! After having worked on the requested areas his wife showed me a bowl with the blockages he had removed. The next day, I had red welts on my body that looked like incisions in the places where he had "operated." Within a week, I noticed a positive shift. In retrospect, I believe that the healing I experienced was due as much to my willingness to change as to Dr. Alex's attention. It was body, mind, and healer working together. Reading Carolyn Myss's work, and my session with Dr. Alex, both inspired me to explore the body-mind connection and how our belief systems can influence our physical well-being.

In my line of work, I hear a lot of stories about different readers and healers, and some frankly odd experiences. Madame Celeste, our local psychic gypsy, is one good example. Gossip has it that she moves from one location to another to stay one step ahead of the law and past clients. I once had a reading with Madame Celeste, the only psychic reader I have encountered who is able to talk on the phone, eat lunch, lay cards, and still give a fairly accurate reading.

However, her accuracy is used to bait the client into what she needs, tapping into their worst fears. She is known for "seeing" curses that needed to be removed. To cast off the curse necessitates more readings, and, thus, more money. One poor woman was given a shopping list of expensive items that Madame Celeste needed as payment in order to remove the curse. It seems that Madame Celeste had a penchant for Chanel scarves. In The World, we take responsibility for our experiences and especially for our destiny. The World is about not turning your power over to Madame Celestes, in whatever profession or walk of life we find them. Whether it is with a psychic, doctor, lawyer, or any professional, establish boundaries regarding what you want to experience.

My work sometimes involves psychic deprogramming. There are those who, unfortunately, go from one psychic to another looking for validation of what they want to hear. The end result can be too many readings and too much information, sometimes conflicting, with the client never taking the time to consider their own thoughts. There comes a time where we must take responsibility for creating our own future, becoming our own authority on the matter. There is fate—the divine plan—and there is free will. The latter plays a big role in the ultimate outcome of one's destiny.

The following are stories that reflect different aspects of The World card. The first is Andie, a makeup artist who was starting to experience recognition and fame in her profession. She had been written up in a well-known glossy magazine and was gaining a national reputation. At the time of her reading, where The World card figured prominently, Andie was contemplating a move from Seattle to New York. Andie had a number of influential contacts in New York and a great portfolio. This was her big career moment, yet she was hesitating.

Andie also had just completed school in Web design as a back-up plan in case her make-up career didn't pan out. In her session, Andie said she was considering forgetting the whole makeup thing. She was on the verge of changing her profession to Web design just when she was on the cusp of success and her dreams were coming true. Andie admitted that she might be scared of success, and especially of the responsibilities involved. Her reading was very clear: encouraging her to make the move and predicting that success was close at hand. The World often relates to career issues, especially in regards to creating an identity for oneself in the world. On this path, it is your time to make things happen. In Andie's case, it suggested that she forget the back up plan and go for her dreams, to celebrate her gifts with others. This path is expansive, meaning that sometimes you have to go outside of your comfort zones to get what you really want.

Another story, this one reflecting Saturn's (the ruler of The World card) influence on the body, concerns Susan, a dancer. Having danced her whole life, she had recently experienced a back injury and couldn't dance any longer. This restriction in her movement indicates the harsh side of Saturn and how it can sometimes represent limitations. Susan had to find a different way to be with her body and the world, to reevaluate her work and change her direction. Susan was heartbroken at having to give up her chosen career. Without dance, she felt like she no longer had an identity she could rely on. This disorientation made her feel as if her whole life was slipping away.

After some soul searching, Susan came up with the idea to teach dance. Her physical limitations led to a whole new expression of her career path. In the process, she learned to be less rigid and more flexible about how she defined both herself and her work. Susan's experience symbolizes one of the many opportunities inherent to The World card—the choice to decide what we do with our limitations. In Susan's case, she made them work for her and her life came full circle in the best sense.

In astrology, Saturn can represent the hard lessons in life, yet if you are willing to work and learn, it can lead you to success. Saturn can be severe but it also gives us the resolve to stick to achieving something. To better understand your World and Saturn connections check out the sign and house placement of Saturn in your birth chart (See page 33).

In The World, we "graduate" to the highest level of our potential. The legendary actress Audrey Hepburn, movie star and icon of beauty and grace, is a wonderful example of a possible component of The

World card: becoming a world ambassador. Hepburn, after a successful film career, marriages, and children, decided later in life to use her influence as a spokesperson for the UNICEF foundation, raising money and building awareness to help the children of the world. Hepburn often said that her most fulfilling work in life was with UNICEF, and it was this even more than her film career that she wanted to be remembered for. By using her gifts in a new way, Audrey Hepburn helped to change the fate of the world.

BIBLIOGRAPHY

Anonymous. *Meditations on the Tarot, A Journey into Christian Hermeticism*. Warwick, N.Y.: Amity House Books, 1985.

Blake, William. "Night." *Songs of Innocence and of Experience*. Paris, France: Trianon Press, 1967.

Brown, Dan. *The Da Vinci Code*. New York: Doubleday, 2003.

Burt, Kathleen. *Archetypes of the Zodiac*. St. Paul, Minn.: Llewellyn, 1990.

Campbell, Joseph, with Bill Moyers. *The Power of Myth*. New York: Archer Books, 1991.

Carson, David, and Jamie Sams. *Medicine Cards: The Discovery of Power Through the Ways of Animals*. Santa Fe, N.M.: Bear and Company, 1988.

Cavendish, Richard. *The Tarot*. New York: Crescent Books, 1986.

Chirlot, J.E. *Dictionary of Symbols*. New York, NY: Dorset Press, 1991.

Chopra, Deepak. *The Seven Spiritual Laws of Success: A Practical Guide to the Fulfillment of Your Dreams*. San Rafael, Calif.: Amber/Allen Publishing and New World Library, 1994.

Choquosh, "Native American Storyteller." *Mountain Astrologer Magazine*. Feb/March 1996.

Crowley, Aleister. *The Book of Thoth: Egyptian Tarot*. York Beach, Maine: Samuel Weiser, 1969.

de Saint-Exupéry, Antoine. *The Little Prince.* Orlando: Harcourt Brace Jovanovich, 1971.

Fairfield, Gail. *Choice Centered Astrology: The Basics.* Smithville, Ind.: Ramp Creek Publishing, 1990.

Freke, Timothy, and Peter Gandy. *The Jesus Mysteries: Was The "Original Jesus" a Pagan God?* New York: Three Rivers Press, 1999.

Gawain, Shakti. *Creative Visualization: Use the Power of Your Imagination to Create What You Want in Your Life.* Novato, Calif.: New World Library, 2002.

Greene, Liz, and Howard Sasportas. *The Luminaries: The Psychology of the Sun and Moon in the Horoscope.* York Beach, Maine: Samuel Weiser, 1992.

Gurian, Michael. *Mothers, Sons & Lovers: How a Man's Relationship With His Mother Affects the Rest of His Life.* Boston: Shambhala Publications, 1993.

Guttman, Ariel, and Kenneth Johnson. *Mythic Astrology: Archetypal Powers in the Horoscope.* St. Paul, Minn.: Llewellyn Publications, 1993.

Hall, Manly P. *The Secret Teachings of All Ages.* Los Angeles: The Philosophical Research Society, 1997.

Hamilton, Edith. *Mythology: Timeless Tales of Gods and Heroes.* New York: Meridian, 1989.

Hay, Louise L. *You Can Heal Your Life.* Santa Monica: Hay House, 1984.

Holy Bible, King James Version. Nashville, Tenn.: Thomas Nelson Publisher, 1984.

Hughes, Langston. "Dream Dust." *Vintage Hughes.* New York: Vintage Books, 2004.

Idemon, Richard. *Through the Looking Glass: A Search for the Self in the Mirror of Relationships.* York Beach, Maine: Samuel Weiser, 1992.

Jung , C.G. *Memories, Dreams and Reflections.* New York: Vintage Books, 1989.

Kornfield, Jack. *Buddha's Little Instruction Book.* New York: Bantam Books, 1994.

Kübler-Ross, Elisabeth. *The Wheel of Life: A Memoir of Living and Dying*. New York: Touchstone, 1997.

Lennon, John. "Imagine." BMG Music Publishing, 1971.

Leo, Alan. *Astrology for All*. Rochester, VT: Destiny Books, 1989.

Lofthus, Myrna. *A Spiritual Approach to Astrology*. Sebastapol, CA: CRCS Publicatons, 1983.

Mauro, Claudia. "This is the poem I can never show you." *Stealing Fire*. Seattle: Whiteaker Press, 1995.

Moore, Thomas. *The Planets Within: The Astrological Psychology of Marsilio Ficino*. Great Barrington, Mass.: Lindisfarne Press, 1990.

Myss, Caroline. *Anatomy of The Spirit: The Seven Stages of Power and Healing*. New York: Three Rivers Press, 1996.

Nhat Hanh, Thich. *The Miracle of Mindfulness: A Manual on Meditation*. Boston: Beacon Press, 1987.

Newton, Michael. *Journey of Souls: Case Studies of Life Between Lives*. St. Paul, Minn.: Llewellyn Publications, 2003.

Nordic, Rolla. *The Tarot Shows the Path*. New York: Samuel Weiser, 1979.

Roberts, Jane. *The Nature of Personal Reality: Specific, Practical Techniques for Solving Everyday Problems and Enriching the Life You Know (A Seth Book)*. San Rafael, Calif.: Amber-Allen Publishing, 1994.

Rowling, J.K. *Harry Potter and The Sorcerer's Stone*. New York: Scholastic Press, 1997.

Rumi. "The Ruins of the Heart." *Love is a Stranger (Translated by Kabir Helminski)*. Putney, Vt: Threshold Books, 1993.

Rumi. "Resurrection Day," "Work in the Invisible." *One Handed Basket Weaving: Poems On The Theme Of Work*. Versions by Coleman Barks, Athens Ga.: Maypop, 1991.

Simpson, Liz. *The Book of Chakra Healing*. New York: Sterling Publishing, 1999.

Stewart, Mary. *The Crystal Cave: Book One of the Arthurian Saga*. New York: Fawcett Columbine, 1970.

Storr, Anthony. *The Essential Jung: Selected Writings*. Princeton, N.J.: Princeton University Press, 1983.

Tolkien, J.R.R. *The Lord of the Rings*. New York: Houghton, Mifflin, 1988.

Tolle, Eckhart. *The Power of Now: A Guide to Spiritual Enlightenment*. Novato, Calif.: New World Library, 1999.

Ueland, Brenda. *If You Want to Write*. St. Paul, Minn.: The Schubert Club, 1984.

Van Praagh, James. *Reaching to Heaven: Spiritual Journey Through Life and Death*. New York: Signet, 2000.

Walker, Barbara. *The Women's Encyclopedia: Myths and Secrets*. New York: Harper Collins, 1983.

Wang, Robert. *The Qabalistic Tarot: A Testbook of Mystical Philosophy*. York Beach, Maine: Samuel Weiser, 1987.

Wing, R.L. *The I Ching Workbook*. New York: Doubleday, 1979.

Wirth, Oswald. *The Tarot of The Magicians*. York Beach, Maine: Samuel Weiser, 1985.

Yogananda, Paramahansa. *Autobiography of a Yogi*. Los Angeles: Self-Realization Fellowship, 1998.

Ziegler, Gerd. *Tarot: the Mirror of the Soul*. York Beach, Maine: Samuel Weiser, 1988.

INDEX

About the Author

Megan Skinner graduated from Washington State University with a Bachelor of Arts degree in communications. She began a career in advertising, climbing the corporate ladder to become a successful account executive with a large Seattle advertising agency. But she found herself called by the Tarot and her psychic gifts to change direction—to help others in understanding their lives from a spiritual and psychic perspective. She has been in private practice ever since, counseling her international client base in spiritual matters for more than 15 years.

Megan resides in Seattle with her cat Merlin where, in addition to writing, she teaches classes and lectures on the Tarot and intuitive development. She has written celebrity profiles and a weekly astrology column for ABCNews.com and has been interviewed on television and radio.

Megan believes in the Tarot's profound ability to reflect back to people their own process and journey. She has written this book to share her perspective on the cards and to tell the stories behind them, to share the stories of her clients in order to help others gain perspective on their own lives through the mysterious teachings of the Tarot.